NOTES FROM A NORTH COUNTRY JOURNAL

ഌരു

Notes from a North Country Journal

Barbara A. Mulvaney

NORTH STAR PRESS OF ST. CLOUD, INC.

Library of Congress Cataloging-in-Publication Data

Mulvaney, Barbara A., 1941-
    Notes from a north country journal / Barbara A.
Mulvaney.—1st ed.
        p. cm.
        ISBN 0-87839-143-6 (alk. paper)
        1. Minnesota—Description and travel. 2. Minnesota—
Pictorial works. 3. Country life—Minnesota. 4. Country life
—Minnesota—Pictorial works. 5. Seasons—Minnesota. 6.
Seasons—Minnesota—Pictorial works. 7. Wilderness areas
—Minnesota. 8. Wilderness areas—Minnesota—Pictorial
works. 9. Natural history—Minnesota. 10. Natural history
—Minnesota—Pictorial works. I. Title.

F610 .M85 2001
977.6'053--dc21   2001030843

Cover photos and all inside photos, unless otherwise
credited, by Barbara Mulvaney

ISBN: 0-87839-143-6

First Edition July 2001

Printed in Canada by Friesens

Published by
North Star Press of St. Cloud, Inc.
P.O. Box 451
St. Cloud, Minnesota 56302

"There is no other door to knowledge
than the door Nature opens;
and there is no truth
except the truths we discover in Nature."
Luther Burbank

Dedicated to all who love nature today
And who nurture the naturalists of tomorrow.

Acknowledgements

Through patience, persistence, and determination, my husband, Bruce, convinced me to abandon my beloved typewriter for a computer. And for this I must thank and gratefully acknowledge his helping me achieve my goal of writing about a subject close to my heart, the North Country.

I would be remiss if I did not mention my parents for their tolerance and encouragement of my varied nature-related interests ranging from collecting butterflies to photography. Although born in Minnesota, I grew up in the shadows of the majestic mountains of the Pacific Northwest where the seed was planted for this book. This idyllic setting created an intense interest in the outdoors for a budding naturalist. My return to Minnesota intensified my appreciation for wilderness.

And to Pepper, fond memories of a wonderful little Shih Tzu, my buddy that slept (and sometimes snored) at my feet during much of the writing for this book. I'm sure he will smile down from that big dog kennel in the sky when his mistress finally achieves the goal of having her book published.

Contents

Introduction

The thought for this book germinated nearly twenty-five years ago while I was snowshoeing on a beautiful winter day in the boreal forests of Minnesota. The evergreen boughs were dolloped with fresh snow consisting of large, dendritic snowflakes sparkling like diamond dust and reflecting a colorful prismatic spectrum of light in the brilliant sunshine. The sky was the deep azure blue of cold winter days characteristically found in the North Country. The beauty of the scene inspired me to attempt to capture the moment with numerous photographs, awakening the desire of wanting to share what I was experiencing. The intent of this book is not only to inspire nature lovers, but to encourage future generations to explore and protect their natural world. It is the hope of the author that the varied subjects will arouse curiosity to pursue and enjoy in more detail nature's many moods and phenomena. One need not have a canoe and portage from lake to lake in the northern forests to experience wilderness. Besides, there are those who would argue that "true" wilderness does not exist, for human beings have left their mark on all but an inaccessible fraction of the planet. By definition, wilderness can be either unsettled land, uncultivated or land allowed to return to a natural state. When

experienced repeatedly throughout seasonal tempera-
ments, wilderness, even with this broader interpretation,
instills in one an inner peace, revitalizing the soul and
fostering an appreciation for the beauty of the universe.
For some, such as myself, the allure of wilderness draws
them into its depth, to explore its mysteries. Having
been fortunate to experience varied definitions of
wilderness, this book has been written to share the
beauty of these encounters through prose, photography,
and enlightenment about the uniqueness of wild places.

NOTES FROM A NORTH COUNTRY JOURNAL

1

Wilderness Cabin

Like the purist who has portaged into the depths of wilderness following the route of voyagers into pristine boreal forests, I, too, have heard the haunting call of the loon and the scream of magnificent eagles. I've enjoyed watching frolicsome otters and become the object of their intense curiosity as they periscope along rugged shorelines. My fishing rod has been challenged by trophy walleye, northern pike, and testy small-mouth bass. I have savored freshly caught lake trout from the cold waters of the North Country. I have witnessed the passage of the seasons and enjoyed the rebirth of endless variations of each. I have stood alone on a lake at midnight in awe of the ephemeral, pulsating waves of phosphorescing green of the aurora borealis, whose ghostly shafts intensify the mystery the Native Americans regarded as their spirited brethren. I have been fortunate to experience all of this because of the comfort of a cabin.

My husband and I knew from our first wilderness experience together that both of us shared a love for the out-of-doors. Shortly after our marriage, we canoed the waters now a part of Voyager's National Park, camped on picturesque islands and soon longed for a permanent place of our own, where whispering, resinous pine grow tall, sky-blue waters caress rocky shorelines, and, when autumnal winds exhale, leaves of birch trees shiver with anticipation before raining gold. We found this pine-scented paradise in a northwoods hideaway accessible by water only, thus giving us the remoteness we had sought previously in Minnesota's Boundary Waters Canoe Area.

As with most adventures, the first is the most memorable. On a Friday after work, with a canoe and a Volkswagen Bug loaded down with everything except a kitchen sink but including our cat, we set off in the darkness for our newly acquired cabin in the wilderness. Although labeled "primitive," we did have electricity and that had an immediate, albeit a temporary, drawback. Our luxuriously white-coated Persian immediately disappeared behind the refrigerator and entwined his body amongst the coils, which resulted in the midnight dismantling of the same to extract the cat now sporting a woodland "camo" coat. This event was one of many to follow that would make our wilderness experience with pets a series of laughs and unpredictable antics.

Our first cabin was a small, simple, plywood structure measuring twenty-four by twenty-four feet and electrified by means of a submarine cable spanning a

Lights from within the cabin cast a glow on the snow.

half mile of lake bottom to the shore hook-up. But that's
where the modernization ended. Out back was the
proverbial outhouse complete with huge, hairy wolf
spiders and mosquitoes. Our one and one-half acre
parcel surveyed and platted in 1927 consisted of 150
feet of rocky shoreline and woodland consisting of red
and white pines, spruce, balsam, and birch. Blueberries
and assorted wildflowers carpeted the understory with
assorted wildflowers nestled amongst the moss-and-
lichen-covered, boulder-strewn hillside. Though our
location was north of the continental divide, the
topography of the watershed allowed flowage to the
south. Without major tributaries flowing north into the
lake, the water was still declared potable by local residents, but with increased activity on the lake, especially
in summer, we have opted to haul in our drinking
water. In summer, our additional water needs are met by
running cold water pumped by an
electric water pump with a pressur-
ized water tank. And in winter we
have icy cold water! After augering a
hole in the lake ice sometimes measuring three feet in thickness, a five-
gallon plastic container is filled and
carried up the hill.

 The old, badly rusted wood-
burning stove that came with the
cabin was a disaster waiting to hap-
pen, so we replaced it with a small
oil burner—on a day when it was at
least twenty below zero. Unbeknownst to us, the flow valve had
been painted over, preventing the
flow of oil to the internal fire pot.
While the cat kept warm by curling
up on a heating pad, I moved to the
fishhouse and kept warm with a catalytic heater. My fingers kept nimble
by catching northern pike in

Harebells that dot the rocky shoreline.

between stringing popcorn for the Christmas tree. Meanwhile, a neighbor joined my semi-frozen husband in the cabin, and between the two of them the problem was identified and corrected.

Going unnoticed, however, was a second problem, a badly maladjusted flue damper. With the ignition of the now free-flowing fuel oil, black clouds of soot erupted, both inside and outside of the cabin. The snow was literally coated with black, and the cabin interior had billions and billions of little soot balls waiting to smudge when the slightest effort was made to subdue them. Need I say what our white Persian cat looked like? Thus began the era of the Big Soot.

But, when the stove burned with that warm, buttery-yellow flame, it was a terrific, cozy companion. However, fuel oil has its limitations, especially at the minus forty degrees Fahrenheit experienced on one of our trips. During brittle cold spells, the wilderness is silenced, and all life seems to be held in suspended animation. So too the fuel oil! Thick, congealed fuel oil will not ooze through copper tubing. The addition of a gasoline catalytic heater temporarily resolved the problem. But it, too, gave in to the cold and ceased to function. A blanket shield brought a few moments of life to the viscous gel before shutting down for the last time. By now the thermometer had broken at forty below, and the power lines snapped. We finally got the message to depart ASAP! But how? The car stood isolated on the barren lake where grease and oil had become winter's super glue. Once again we revived the catalytic, placed it under the car's oil pan to warm the engine oil, replaced the battery, which had been removed twenty-four hours earlier to the semi-warmth of the cabin, and drove across the lake on square tires. This was perhaps the coldest trip we have experienced.

By contrast some of our summer days have easily exceeded ninety-five degrees. The paradoxical weather prize goes to early April—the ice is still two feet thick, the temperature may surpass seventy degrees, butterflies come out of hibernation, and it's possible for a thunderstorm to flood the lake surface.

Though our first cozy cabin gave us many happy memories, we choose to move five miles to the north end of the lake to a larger cabin and a slightly less inhabited and definitely more scenic area with lichen-covered, jagged balsalt and granite rock outcroppings. We gained a fireplace and, unbeknownst to us, a nesting pair of eagles on the island about one-eight mile from the cabin, but we gave up electricity. This move like-wise gave us closer access to a portage into rugged wilderness lakes and, most important, to the deepest one, containing lake trout. The latter lake comprises a splendid example of the Canadian Shield, rock scoured out by retreating glaciers thousands of years ago, giving birth to very deep, cold-water lakes.

A discussion of our cabin in the wilderness would not be complete without commenting on wildlife. Most endearing of the critters are the small ones. With the addition of various feeders, chipmunks, squirrels, and chickadees as well as the friendly gray jays eat from our hand. Winter allows us to witness bird behavior not readily viewed during the remainder of the year, and the omnipresent chickadees always at the cabin, greeting us upon arrival, gave us a lesson in nature's sometime cruel scheme. For example, we were delighted to have a flur-ry of black-capped chickadees dine on our deck. Then the inevitable happened; a window collision left one of the chickadees dazed. Before it could recover, it was subjected to repeated blows to the head by other chick-adees. When a tint of blood appeared, I intervened and scooped the little ball of fluff up and put it inside a cov-ered box until it recovered. To me, this epitomized the phrase "survival of the fittest" for the rare treat of sun-flower seeds in the far north. Another window collision knocked a ruffed grouse out, as they say, stone cold. Fortunately, I was just several steps ahead of our golden retriever and carried the limp bird back to the wood-shed to recover enough to fly off in the opposite direction from the cabin. Unlike other rescuees, the fox sparrow found frozen to a twig at the water's edge in late fall was reluctant to accept its freedom. Returning from an afternoon outing, I found the hapless creature and broke the branch upon which its feet were frozen and brought the otherwise very alert bird into the warmth of the cabin. After the icy entrapment had melted, I took the bird outside and, removing it from the box, waited for it to leave. It just sat on my finger, refusing to take flight into the cold air.

High summer in the north is very special indeed. Dawn comes early at this time of the year, revealing the morning mist rising silently from the lake surface with apparitional grace. Ripples consisting of multiconcentric rings form as a small-mouth bass rises to the unfortunate insect landed on the water. The rapidly growing merganser ducklings frolic in the shallows as they dart after small minnows. The quiet of the morning is interrupted as a loon laughs at the sun trying to burn through the gauzy mist, making the air humid and pungent with the essence of summer's perfume. The overnight rain provides a spa of water on the foliage in which a hummingbird first imbibes, then flutters, dipping its wings and tossing micro-droplets over its body for its morning shower. I remind myself that this is what owning a cabin is about as I sip a second of cup of coffee before the rest of the lake residents awaken.

A chipmunk overindulges on corn.

As friendly as the chickadees are (most of the time), chipmunks get the award for downright brazenness. One of the more comical scenes: a bold chipmunk sitting on the rim of the dog's food bowl stealing large kibble chunks literally inches from the dog's nose. Its cheeks swelled bilaterally, like a massive case of mumps. Loaded to capacity, the striped charmer scurried off to hide individual pieces throughout the forest and came back to repeat the sequence over and over. This miniature thief emptied the collie's bowl and curiously mesmerized the gentle dog lying with her food dish tucked between her paws! We still laugh remembering the juvenile chipmunk that unrelentingly pursued a northern leopard frog as it vaulted across the forest floor, always just a jump ahead of the bewildered rodent. Sometimes just after dusk, a special treat would be the sighting of northern flying squirrels in the feeders enjoying sunflower seeds. These "fairy-diddles" dined, their flight capes nearly invisible when contracted and folded close to their bodies. Their huge, black and limpid eyes made them even more endearing, and I often wished I could reach out and stroke the soft, fawn-colored fur of these nocturnal sprites.

Though mink are considered fierce fighters and sometimes bad tempered, they have been a constant source of entertainment for us whether performing acro-batics off the fish-cleaning table, tiptoeing along the boat gunnel or balancing precariously on the rim of the fish refuse bucket.

Human encounters with striped skunks have been amusing; however, dog provoking encounters invariably left the unmistakable aroma of mercaptans—

Ripples create a jagged moonbeam "bolt" as the curtain of night draws closed.

the main ingredient of skunk salvos—lingering in the air
. . . and on the golden retriever. Often times, the only
source of skunk perfume eradication we had on hand
was leftover MacDonald's ketchup packets and Prell
shampoo. The combination was barely effective and
totally disgusting to a proud hunting dog!

On a rare occasion a sleek, pine marten
scampered across my path at dusk, but a more lasting
memory of marten activity was the total destruction of
our tubular sunflower seed feeder. Its skilled arboreal
climbing ability allowed one dirty-footed thief to
disassemble the feeder adjacent to our kitchen window.
All that remained after the raid were multiple paw prints
and nose smears on the windowpane.

Coyotes have been nearly apparitional as they
vanish into dense alders in the fading light of sundown,
and the only spectral evidence of timber wolves has
been their huge paw prints on the snow-covered lake in
winter. Moose, too, and I think fortunately, have been
elusive; every fall I hear of someone getting "treed" by a
rutting moose just north of our cabin. Red fox in contrast are very evident in winter and display comical
curiosity as they roam the lake ice, sometimes sitting
and staring at the cabin.

Deer are most evident in winter as they use the
frozen lake surface for easier travel. Once, as my
husband stood on the lake ice fishing in an unusually
dense fog, he sensed a presence and thought he heard
something behind him. Calling out, there was no
response, but later when he checked where the snow-
crunching sound had come from, there were the
unmistakable dainty, heart-shaped hoof prints of one
very curious deer having approached within one hundred feet!

Two medium size mammals, although both have
endearing qualities, give us the most frustration. Otters,
those streamlined clowns of the water world steal our
fish and repeatedly raid minnow buckets. It doesn't matter if our catch is on a stringer or in the locked livebox,

the owners of those dexterous fingers have had some mighty fine meals at our expense! And, if we interrupt one of their many raids, we face ferocious growls and hisses.

The occasional porcupine waddling into the yard just after dusk only requires that we make sure the dogs are secured. More drastic measures were necessitated when a porcupine with tunnel vision was bent on destroying our woodshed. For some reason it had an odd penchant for our plywood woodshed recently stained with a wood preservative. His dining hour was more than fashionably late, and it was downright unacceptable! Several times, about two o'clock in the morning, its gnawing on the corner of the woodshed reverberated throughout the forest, rudely awakening us and rousting my groggy husband out into darkness to dissuade the addict.

Black bears, until recently have never presented a serious problem, perhaps because we always have owned a dog. They avoid us while mildly harassing other area cabin owners. In the last year, however, during our absence, our fishhouse has served both as scratching post and teething ring for a cantankerous bruin.

Fishing the deep, cool waters of the far north has produced trophy northern pike up to twenty-two pounds, and walleyes weighing nearly twelve pounds have been caught through the ice, while four-pound small-mouth bass have challenged summer fishing rods. Silver muskie occasionally followed our lures or live-bait to the surface and sometimes have boldly slashed our hooked game fish. A yearly ritual of courting muskies takes place in our bay. It's exciting to see these huge fish swim side by side into the shallow sandy bay oblivious to lures or humans gazing from the dock or while walking several feet away on the sand beach.

But the real reward of fishing pristine lakes is to catch those beautiful, silver colored lake trout. Each open-water trip presents new challenges, but to catch a lake trout in the winter on a contraption called an airplane jig requires skill and just a bit more luck. Trout from these relatively pure waters often have the deep orange flesh typical of native trout as opposed to yellow-tinted flesh of nursery stock often caught in the Great Lakes. Whether using heavy or light tackle, it is a thrill to catch a "laker" that pulls every trick in the book attempting to throw the hook. Twisting, spinning and head tossing maneuvers occasionally win for them their freedom. Several times as we have reeled in a small lake trout performing such an exhibition on the lake surface, both either an adult or an immature eagle has flown down in an attempt to grab our hooked fish, fortunately withdrawing at the last moment. Events like this make every trip individual and memorable.

Nature continually reveals new facets that amaze and delight us, causing us to marvel at how closely interwoven the web of her design has been conceived and how fragile it can be, thus strengthening the concept that we must all be stewards of the land if others are to share the same joy of wilderness in the future. So, come Friday afternoon when Minneapolitans make a mass exodus for the North Country and the inquiry is called out, "Goin' up north?" our reply is always the same enthusiastic Minnesota phrase: "You betcha!"

Reflecting a silver patina, waves skip across the lake surface.

2

North Country Spring

It happens the same every year. With childlike anticipation, I flip the calendar to the month of March and there it is—March 20—spring! Not only is the celestial event a time in the northern hemisphere when the sun crosses the vernal equinox, March is the month of Mother Nature's gentle awakening from her long winter nap. I start yet another log book to record daily, subtle hints of spring, which wears a varied wardrobe to demonstrate her moods and comes in many disguises. Ideally, she will sail in under an azure sky on warm southern zephyrs, advancing at a rate of twelve miles a day. The soothing dripping of melting snow forms small rivulets and, warmed by the heat of the sun, combine to form the vital aroma of damp humus. Nomadic evening grosbeaks, those beautiful, gold, brown, and white birds of the north, possess the ingenuity to sip droplets of melting snow as it spills over the edge of our cabin roof. In the warming rays of early April, aspects of photoperiodism—the response to lengthening daylight—are in evidence as female grosbeaks increasingly perform

A member of the finch family, this male evening grosbeak sports its spring finery of gold, brown, with white on black wings.

wing-quivering postures, which in turn causes males to respond with courtship feeding typical of passerines.

With moderating temperatures, moss clumps become exposed on southwest facing rocks and absorb melting snow like bright green sponges. Where snow is deeper, footprints become tombs for snow fleas, which became active when the temperature reaches twenty-seven degrees Fahrenheit. These members of the springtail family measure only a millimeter and look like flecks of black pepper. The warmth of the sun coaxes hibernating butterflies from their winter somnolence, and, often, the mourning cloak is the first to rouse. Puddles forming on the lake surface become mirrored images of the shoreline and sky, creating a beautiful picture.

Impatient ruffed grouse can be heard drumming, perhaps while sitting upon a log facing south, catching the warm spring rays. Ravens call overhead, and, although already paired in March, an occasional couple may be seen in the aerial nuptial flight, tumbling toward the earth at a dizzy pace. The welcome cry of the bald eagle is heard, and they, too, have completed their cart-wheeling acts of courtship and are busy refurbishing last year's nest. Migrating flocks of redpoll finches alight in the tree tops of birches. In the morning light, their crimson caps glow like forgotten Christmas ornaments. These birds of the Arctic are unique in that they have the ability to store seeds in tiny throat pouches, allowing food to be consumed at their leisure or after dusk. The dulcet treetop twittering of song sparrows at sundown promises summer. And not to be overlooked are the male woodpeckers rapping a reverberating rhapsody throughout the woodland, establishing territories and informing the ladies of their location. Only the most resonant tree will do and, if one to their taste is not available, use of metal poles has been documented. Increasingly, numerous slate-colored juncos just arriving from southern wintering grounds are ravenous diners at the millet feeder. And although the "fee-bee" song of male black-capped chickadees has been practiced since

January, the feathered mites have now perfected their mating call, and it is heard throughout the forest in the stillness of morning. As vocal as the chickadees are now, the great horned owls are silent compared to a month ago when they were establishing nesting territories. Starting just after sundown, the females higher pitched five-part call was answered by the slower and deeper tone of the male. Now, the female incubates her two to three eggs during March snowstorms. The blue-jays are grouped now, looking spiffy in their blue-and-white spring attire, but the best composition they can sing sounds like a pump handle. The gray jays are glutinous gourmands that snitch anything and everything from the bird-feeding tray to feed their young that may hatch as early as March. Left-over food is stashed in crevices, secured in place with thick saliva.

Hazelnut blossoms appear with minute petals looking like the scarlet tentacles of Caribbean Sea anemones. In the hardwood forests, scarlet cup fungi emerge from the damp humus, glowing like miniature beacons nestled among last autumn's leaves. Red oaks, the last to shed autumn's leaves, begin to release them, and the rosy-red maple buds begin to swell, as do the buds on the aspens near the shore, bringing promise of future green lushness. Overnight, as the temperature drops, crystalline icicles are held in suspended animation. The unfortunate spider blown onto the lake ice will become temporarily entombed until the warm rays of morning light free it. From the edge of the marsh, velvety pussy willows peek out from their dark winter caps.

A raccoon may emerge from its winter tree den to sit like a Buddha, propped up against the tree bole luxuriating in the warmth of the sun. Tufts of white-tailed deer hair are scattered about as winter coats of gray are discarded for summer shades of reddish brown. Even last year's burdock seed heads contain deer hair, which in turn becomes entangled in our dog's ruff. Antlers, too, have been shed, though we have observed bucks as late as March still with antlers and scraping against saplings as they did during the fall rut. Snowshoe hares have become dappled with brown now, and the ermine or short-tailed weasel is also exchanging its cloak of winter white for summer brown. The landscape near the marsh is pock marked with tracks of courting snowshoe hares. In the glow of moonlight, the does, while standing on hind feet, strike punches like miniature boxers, fending off the unwanted attention of overly amorous suitors. Observers in the past, having witnessed these pixilating matches, often erroneously described the scene as "The Dance of

Boreal forest reflection created by the spring melt of winter snows.

the Snowshoe Hare." On a warm day, eastern chipmunks emerge to visit the birdfeeder, looking for sunflower seeds to add to their dwindling winter cache; they know a late spring storm could send them once again into a torpid state. Red squirrels, too, are opportunists and indulge in the high-protein seed.

Like a mirror, puddles on the frozen lake surface reflect the shoreline.

15

As the snow cover continues to diminish, the ground beneath the occasional balsam tree is noticeably littered with approximately four-inch lengths of branch tips. One of the two culprits to sever these tender tips months previously is the red squirrel, which finds the phloem just beneath the bark barely nutritious but which helps sustain them through rough winters. Porcupines are sloppy diners and are responsible for dropping many small branches as well, thus providing a treat for deer and snowshoe hares.

Many animals crave salt, and deer are certainly no exception. One March, we discovered a muskrat house nearly demolished. The area was surrounded with hundreds of the dainty, heart-shaped prints of deer. Actually, the house was what is termed a "feeding" house, where muskrats come out of the water in summer to consume water plants. This structure is about half the size of the main lodge. The remains of the feeding hut revealed starchy cattail tubers as well as leafy aquatic vegetation. Aquatic plants contain sodium counts as high as 10,000 parts per million, and perhaps the deer took advantage of this readily available source of salt along one of their main night travel lanes. Given the opportunity on a winter outing across our pond, the family dog consumes these same salty remnants of vegetation. Moose have been observed along northern highways seeking salt from road chemicals. Birds, too—such has grosbeaks, finches, and crossbills—peck amongst the roadside gravel in March, perhaps to obtain calcium from calcium chloride residue.

Spring ice fishing not only produces occasional fish but is also a source of entertainment for the wildlife enthusiast. Once, a gray jay was attracted to the red plastic tip-up flag in the augured fishing hole just inches from the fisherman. The inquisitive bird cocked its head, examined the flag from all angles and, upon deciding it was inedible, seemingly finessed its error by taking a long, slow drink of water. This behavior was not unusual since these friendly birds not only associate the color red in autumn with food offered at deer camps, but red also often signifies a snack from a deer kill.

Shortly before sundown, as I angled for lake trout on a northern lake in March, the surrounding forest became a theater for the performing barred owls as they established their territories by vocalizing their

The barred owl, along with the barn owl, are unique in that they have dark eyes. All other owls have yellow eyes.

unique call characterized as: "Who cooks for you?" "Who cooks for you all?" Another time, a hole cut in the ice provided not only delight for an otter but an easy exit from the frozen lake. The activity must have alerted the troops, for soon there were four otters cavorting and belly sliding along the shore. Then like an explosion of playful kittens, they scrambled back to the hole in their loping fashion before plopping out of sight.

Crows and ravens find fishing holes a delicatessen of discarded minnows and often approach the bounty with amusing stalking tactics. Late one evening, while I checked on our minnow bucket on the frozen lake, I nearly stumbled on an opportunistic striped skunk as it searched for ice-fishing tidbits. Fortunately after stamping its feet, it did a dainty pirouette and finished its thorough inspection of the area before disappearing into the forest. As it left, it glanced back at me, probably upset I had intruded on its night-time foraging. Ice break up ends ice fishing and promises a new season.

As the sun arcs even higher during the day, the plasticity of the snow allows it to slide off the metallic roof of the wood shed in one large cascading blanket. Throughout the forest, dollops of snows plop to the ground, relieving winter's weight from weary branches. Shallow bays begin to thaw along the shore, and insects scurry on the sun-warmed lake bottom. The aroma of warm pine resin permeates the air, evoking pleasant summer memories soon to be relived. Crows, having begun their migration north, become increasingly more numerous; a few great blue herons straggle northward as do the loquacious male redwing blackbirds returning to the marshes. And when Canada geese noisily defend nesting territories in late March, one gets the feeling that spring's arrival is official!

The tranquil beauty of early spring opens the door for the boisterous and bold. Now, a riot of pastels will follow as spring progresses into its final stage and in turn gives way to the dramatic colors of summer.

3

Summer Delights

When does summer arrive? Does it simply begin with a date on a calendar, indicating the arrival of the longest day of the year, June twenty-first? Summer's advent has many traditional interpretations, but for me summer truly happens in the north when bogs become alive with blooming plants. Technically speaking, however, this region, not being very acidic but containing peatmoss, is best described as fen rather than bog. Here, the luxuriously spongy carpet of sphagnum moss is home to delicate orchids ranging in shades of white to the striking pinks of such plants as dragon's mouth and grass pinks, which are the epitome of northwoods elegance. Summer is when one can let the bog juices ooze into tennis shoes while exploring the domain of insectivorous pitcher plants and inhaling the fragrant white blossoms of Labrador tea. On the diminutive scale is the carnivorous sundew plant nestled among floating mats of mosses. Blooming white cotton grasses backlit by the summer sun create a spectral haze, and the delicate, exquisitely soft tamarack needles clinging to their previous winter-barren branches, further enhances this northern ethereal scene.

The awakening of the peatlands across the north brings an abundance of insect activity, most notable the mosquito. The larva of one species (*Wyeomyia smithii*) actually over winters in the "horn" of the pitcher plant. By contrast to the relatively drab, pesky mosquito, when the eastern tiger swallow-tail butterfly emerges from its chrysalis, it becomes the daytime beauty of the wood-

Like liquid sunshine, the beautiful eastern tiger swallow-tail butterfly floats through forest glades sampling the nectar from many flowers.

lands as well as a visitor to blooming bog flowers. With its four-inch wingspan and appendages on the hind wings ending in half-inch tails, it glides like liquid sunshine through the forest, stopping to imbibe nectar-laden flowers. Once, while I was only able to fumble with my camera, one of these yellow-and-black-stripped beauties visited the maroon flowers of several pitcher plants to create a beautiful visual memory.

Warm, humid summer nights belong to the world of moths, and nothing is more beautiful than the

Nearly translucent, the pale green luna moth has just emerged from its cocoon and will live but a few short days.

-legant, pale-green Luna moth with an average
wingspan of five inches and striking, long tails on the
hind wings. Like other members of the family of
Saturniidae, these moths also have no mouth parts and
ve less than a week. Hawkmoths, so called because
hey can hover like a raptor, are often characterized by
unique geometric patterns on their wings and dart about
ke crazed bumblebees feeding on nectar-laden honey-
uckle blossoms with their two-inch long, hollow pro-
oscis.

The Houdinis of the night, and sometimes, cloudy days, are members of the genus of moths known as underwings. When some of these moths alight on a tree trunk, their beautiful orange to scarlet hind wings disappear beneath the bark-colored forewings. If pursued by a predator, they will startle and often elude the enemy by flashing their brilliantly colored underwings. The beautiful underwing species of *Catocala* have patterns of demarcation that camouflage perfectly with mottled birch bark or geometrically patterned shades that seem to disappear when they rest with their wings closed on various conifer boles. This group of moths can readily be attracted by an old technique called "sugaring." After combining sugar with stale beer and a bit of rum, one "paints" this mixture on various tree trunks at dusk. Several hours later, the beam of a flashlight will reveal numerous moths imbibing the sweet treat, and many will be underwings. Oranges that attract orioles by day seem to be especially enticing for underwing moths at night that actually prefer the fruit slightly fermented.

The warm month of July means that the same island that is home to the bald eagles will be the realm of the diminutive falcons identified as merlins. The fledglings from this year's nest will again claim the northern aspect of the island as their territory, and the American kestrel-like "klee-klee-klee" cry will find them perched in the same gnarled snag at the water's edge. With dusky brown backs and heavily streaked breasts, these jay-sized raptors have both delighted and amazed us as they go into swift, horizontal power dives to snatch unsuspecting dragonflies darting over the lake surface. As these birds of prey mature, these attacks will hone their skill to take small birds. For now, when a victor returns to enjoy its dragonfly breakfast, it is quickly joined by its siblings vying for part of the prize, clamoring like rambunctious toddlers.

Ah, what summer evening would not be complete without the haunting call of the loon, the embodiment of wilderness so many of us eagerly anticipate when we, too, make the return migration to northern lakes. One of my favorite summer events is watching loon chicks, those fluffy, sooty-gray, floating bedroom slippers! However, their buoyant down coat has limitations and inhibits the ability to submerge during the first week of life. Like defiant tennis balls, they bounce back to the surface of the water when attempting to join their parents in a dive. Though the loon has four main calls, the wail, tremolo, hoot, and the yodel, most of us are most familiar with the tremolo. The tremolo interestingly is the only call of the four that can be uttered during flight. Of the combinations of vocalizations, the most interesting is "chorusing," which occurs in the spring and is thought to be used for territorial establishment. Once, while camping on the shores of a lake appropriately named Loonhaunt, we were overwhelmed by the continuous haunting calls of numerous loons throughout the night. Later, realizing that this performance took place the last week of May, we learned this was indeed the period for staking out territories.

With the approach of autumn, loons exchange their dapper tuxedo colors for drab dark-gray plumage and become mute until the following spring. The molt-ing of breeding plumage to traveling duds is shocking to discover on a calm lake when it can become littered with thousands of tiny feathers from a large migration congregation. The adults will be the first to migrate, leaving behind their chicks, which stay until freeze-up of northern lakes. Gathering in large groups, their muted voices sound not unlike little whimpering puppies and with a late summer morning mist shrouding their form, the experience is almost apparitional.

As I check through my journal and come upon the words: "A two blueberry pie vacation," I have fond memories. Not only for the bounty of this midsummer treat, but because of all the other factors making the seasonal collection of a bucket of blueberries special.

Forget the mosquitoes, gnats, horse and deer flies, bear scat, and a ninety-five-pound golden retriever flopping on the bushes where you are picking and nearly spilling the bucket. Rather, watch for butterflies, especially the banded purple butterfly, which is attracted to blueberry-laden bear dung! With nearly a three-inch wingspan, these velvety-black butterflies with broad white bands on both fore and hind wings extract salt or amino acids with their proboscis while lined up side by side, oblivious to an audience. The fortunate blueberry picker to

The beautiful, somewhat rare orchid of the bog has the unflattering name of dragon's mouth.

The pattern of "eyes" on the hind wings of a blinded sphinx moth creates a paradox.

find a patch in a burned-over area might also be in the company of the striking pink of fireweed blossoms. These wildflowers, the first to germinate after a fire because of their ability to lie dormant for years, not only cover the scars of a burn but produce an extensive root system, preventing erosion of exposed soil. And, who can deny that the first handful of berries isn't the tastiest of the season? For me, the blending of the aroma of ripe blueberries and hot pine resin creates one of the basic ingredients of a northwoods summer.

After the bucket of blueberries has provided breakfast berries 'n' cream, fritters, and pancakes, it's time for the pie! Simplest is best when it comes to making a blueberry pie, and my fail-proof recipe takes just minutes to prepare. Ingredients for the pie crust consists of two cups of flour, a teaspoon of salt, one-half cup cooking oil and one-quarter cup milk. Stir together with a fork and split the dough in half before rolling out between two sheets of waxed paper. For the filling, combine one cup of sugar, four tablespoons of flour, half a teaspoon salt (optional), a pinch each of nutmeg and cinnamon. Mix with four cups of berries before adding to the pie shell. Bake in an oven at 400 degrees for thirty-five to forty minutes. This pie, for me, captures the essence of summer.

If daylight belongs to butterflies and night belongs to the moths, then dusk, for a brief moment in summer, belongs to the mayflies. Then mayflies dance. Though I have read numerous accounts of mayfly hatches that have literally greased highways and bridges near large bodies of water, only once have I witnessed the spectacle of courtship. One fact has become apparent; mayflies don't always hatch in May! During the early hours of a calm evening in June while we were fishing, the performance of a lifetime was about to unfold. We became increasing aware of numerous pale yellow, delicate mayflies and suddenly we were caught up in an undulating wave of golden wings. Higher and higher they swirled, forming a cloud over the nearby island. As each female mated, she returned to the surface of the water to eject about 1,500 eggs, and, abruptly, the dance was over. The ballerinas of the dusk had accomplished their mission in life. Soon their bodies littered the lake surface, becoming a gourmet feast for hungry bass. The eggs sank immediately to the bottom. Two years would pass before this progeny would appear for the next dance.

As the curtain of night descends even further, the glittering diamond-dust sparkle of thousands of fireflies over marshy areas flashes a Morse code for attracting mates. Actually, only the male firefly flits through the night air while the ladies wait on the ground to receive the right message before flashing an acknowledging invitation. Not only does the adult have the ability to "glow" but also the larva, hence the term "glow worm." When the combination of a protein called luciferin and the enzyme luciferinase is mixed with oxygen, it produces a pulsating glow. But not all that twinkles is a prospective mate. There are carnivorous impostors that have managed to duplicate codes and lie in wait for an evening meal of an unsuspecting amorous male firefly.

Nothing is utterly more charming than to witness the courtship of the ruby-throated hummingbird. Looking quite dapper as the setting sun intensified its

iridescent plumage and especially the blazing red patch
known as the gorget, one male we observed was
possessed with "dance fever." Nothing like doing the
"Pendulum Swing" for a lady fair; throw in a few high
pitched squeaks, and she'll swoon. Well, maybe. We
have witnessed this dance several times, but though the
ladies sat politely, they didn't seem overly impressed. In
fact some were more interested in returning to the
hummingbird feeder for a nightcap. The wide arc aerial
display as the male swings to and fro repeatedly is
accompanied with a hum. This feathered mite is our
only eastern hummingbird and is readily attracted to
hummingbird feeders from May until the first week or
two of September. Hummingbirds are particularly
numerous in the coniferous north, where abundant
birch trees intersperse among the dark green of spruce
and pine. The "sapwells" in the birch trees are the
drawing cards and are created by a member of the
woodpecker family called the yellow bellied sapsucker.
Drilling birch boles with numerous precise holes causes
sap to flow, providing hummingbirds not only sugary
syrup but with insects as well, attracted to the sticky
treat. Hummingbirds often stake claim to area
"sapwells," probably to help satiate a high metabolic
rate that requires them to feed almost nonstop throughout daylight hours.

As summer wanes, bird migrations are already
underway, and fading August flowers form seed
capsules—future progeny and next year's blooms.
Decreasing sunlight hours stimulates hoarding instincts
in forest creatures, and piles of hazelnut shells are
already evident. As the refuse pile grows, the
disappearance of rosehips is noted as chipmunks collect
this sought-after nutritional treat for their winter larder.
Of the 125 species of goldenrod, an occasional bold
plant blossoms, setting the pace for others to silently
herald the inevitable approach of fall.

A giant puffball. For size comparison, the author's watch was placed on top this large, edible mushroom.

King of the mycological world, the morel mushroom found in the spring is also Minnesota's state mushroom.

4

Incredible Edibles

In a venture through a field or to the neighborhood woodlot, chances are pretty good that a varied supermarket of edible delectables can be found. Vitamin-enriched, chemical free, nutritional, tasty and free for the taking, this harvest only requires the investment of exercise outdoors throughout three of Minnesota's four seasons. For the fourth season, while next year's vegetation and mycelium lie dormant beneath a mantel of white, enjoy a spicy wilderness tea on a bright winter day in the North Country.

A gem of a discovery in late May would be finding the state mushroom of Minnesota known as the morel, one of "the foolproof four," a label created by Clyde M. Christensen, University of Minnesota professor of plant pathology. Also called the sponge mushroom, the morel is so distinctive in appearance that once a picture of one is seen in a book, it is easily recognizable in the woodlands. Averaging two to four inches in height, this pointed, crinkled-capped mushroom, ranging from tan to brown in color, is often found at the base of, or where elm trees once grew. They have also been found in basswood forests, old orchards, and sometimes in amongst prickly ash. This prince of the mushroom world is an epicurian delight fit for a king and is easily prepared by simply wiping the mushroom clean of any soil or leaf debris, slicing length wise and sautéing in butter for several minutes. A light seasoning of salt is all that is necessary to appreciate the delicate flavor. Surprisingly, nutritionally speaking, mushrooms may contain as much as four percent protein and are mineral rich.

About the same time morels are fruiting, the wild asparagus spears may be found. Identifying the previous year's two- to three-foot brown stalk about a half inch in circumference is the best way to find the plants. The asparagus tips are visible at the base of the plant and look identical to domestic asparagus. That's because it is the same; there is no separate species of wild asparagus. It is believed that birds scatter the seed from cultivated asparagus, and now this delicacy is found all over the United States. In autumn, the feathery foliage of mature stalks turns a golden color with bright red seed capsules. This is the time to make a mental note of the location of the plants for the next spring harvest.

Wild violets are not only pretty, but both the leaves and the flowers are edible. The dark green leaves are an excellent source of both vitamin A and C, having more of both than many vegetables found in the grocery store. A one-half cup of violets leaves, for example, will provide as much vitamin C as four average oranges and exceeds the daily requirement of vitamin A. The leaves can be cooked and seasoned like spinach or torn into small pieces as an addition to a tossed salad. The blossoms have a high ascorbic acid value and can be used in salads or as a unique garnish.

The fixings for spring salads range from watercress, found throughout the state in shallow streams, to wild mustard, plantain, young leaves from dandelions, and wild lettuce—or compass plant as it is sometimes called—and even common clover combine to make a healthy wilderness salad. The buds or blossoms of any of these plants impart additional flavor and character.

Summer is a marvelous season filled with an assortment of easily procurable fruits. But, when it comes to finding a versatile vegetable, head for the swamp where the ubiquitous cattail has much to offer. While the plant is still young, perhaps no more than two feet high, "Cossack asparagus" can be gathered. Taking hold and twisting the inside leaves will reveal the compact, white, inner portion of the plant. When eaten raw or as an addition to a salad, it lends a delicate cucumber flavor. The bloom, before or even slightly after it has left the sheath of dark green leaves, can be boiled and, with the addition of butter and salt, tastes very much like young corn. When the blooms just start to mature they are encased in a massive amount of pollen that can quickly be gathered by tapping the cattail heads into a bucket. This makes a very light pancake flour when mixed equally with regular flour and lends a golden color to pancakes. There are numerous accounts of flour made from the starchy roots as well.

Lamb's quarter, sometimes known as goosefoot, is actually a wild spinach and is readily found in waste areas along country roads and, in my case, always pops up as a weed in my flower or vegetable garden. It's one of the occasional plants that is entirely edible, top to bottom, and from early spring to the first frost of fall. It is regarded as one of the more edible wild greens, for unlike supermarket spinach, the tender tops have no strong flavor. The leaves can also be eaten raw and torn into small pieces as an addition to a salad. Even the seeds are edible, and Indians once ground them into a meal; granted the seeds are minute, but one plant may have as many as 75,000 of them!

There are many other natural greens to be enjoyed, though often the plants are regarded as weeds. They are free for the discovery, chemically untainted and, certainly, not genetically altered. Recently, in early July when the milkweed blossoms were in the tight-bud stage, I got brave, dug out my Euell Gibbons field guide edition of *Stalking the Wild Asparagus* and turned to the chapter on "Milkweeds." I followed the instructions for cooking the unopened buds. And voilá—they were deli-

A sulfur shelf mushroom growing in a Minnesota forest in August.

cious, having a unique flavor, somewhat a blend of several garden vegetables. With the milkweed plant slowly disappearing from the countryside due to loss of habitat, I would hope any reader interested in cooking with plants from the wild do so in only small amounts. The only reason I experimented was that the plants grew in the middle of our farm road and the truck tires would have crushed the unopened flower heads. If the milkweed goes, so do the beautiful monarch butterflies, mentioned elsewhere.

Another plant that provides flavor to any dish comes not only from above ground but beneath. The wild prairie onion is found throughout the state and is readily identifiable by the erect umbel or flower head in shades of pale to rosy pink atop a one foot stalk, often found blooming in August. Though the slender leaves may be used like garden chives in a salad, the bulb lends itself to many dishes and is easily substituted for the domestic variety of garden onion.

As the month of August progresses, so do the chances for finding the remaining members of the "the foolproof four" mushroom cadre. In the hardwood forests, where oak and basswood trees grow, one may be fortunate to discover the sulphur shelf mushroom. This is a bracket fungus, growing in masses either attached to living tree trunks or at the base of or on old stumps or logs. As the name implies, this mushroom has a sulfur color, ranging from golden yellow to orange. Removing no more than two-thirds of the tender outer portion will insure the selection of the most tender part and an unbelievable taste treat. Cut or torn into small pieces, shaken in a small amount of flour and sautéed in margarine or butter, the flavor and texture is comparable to chicken.

Puffballs, though they can be found in summer, are most numerous in the fall. They range in size from the giants, which grow as big as volleyballs, to a species less than the diameter of a quarter. It is the smaller variety that we find the tastiest, but, with this size, one must be sure to slice the mushroom in half, not only to make sure there is no internal discoloration but to insure that there is *no* stem present. Puffballs do not have stems at any stage, but some poisonous varieties can resemble the puffball shape externally in their stages of early growth. I suggest that would-be mushroom gathers obtain a good identification text and/or join a local mycological society to learn which species are safe to eat. As with the previous mushrooms, simply slicing and sautéing is the best way to enjoy the delicate flavor of the puffball. These mushrooms also can be sliced and added raw to a green salad for a special taste treat.

The fourth member of this elite group of mushrooms is the shaggy mane, a member of the inky cap family, and is as distinct in appearance as the morel. Again a good picture of one is an adequate tool to be able to correctly identify this mushroom. Standing from three to six inches tall, this somewhat rounded, pointed-capped mushroom is white with shaggy, loosely overlapping scales. Though reported to be prevalent spring through fall, we have found September the most reliable month to find them.

As free and diverse as the entrées are, so are the beverages—wilderness teas I like to call them. Some are extremely simple. Pluck a dried clover blossom head or two, rub them between the palms to dislodge the florets from the stem, place in a cup, add boiling water and steep several minutes. Often though, as with basswood tea, it's best to select the flowers in their prime and let the blossoms dry before sealing in a jar to hold in the flavor. Then some wintry day, add a cup of boiling water to one tablespoon of the nectar-laden blossoms and savor the essence of summer once again. This is one of many teas that are not only sweet and fragrant but, as herbalist have known for years, have medicinal value as well.

Numerous teas can be made from any of the mint family, including catnip. But if there is a feline in residence, one of the approximately seventy percent of cats attracted to catnip, this critter is going to be all over the counter, looking for the source of the catnip aroma. Our Persian cat proved this truism. Wintergreen is the exception to most teas whose leaves are dried and stored for later use. Its unique favor is lost in drying, and the leaves should be used shortly after picking. The best flavor comes from the young leaves, and tearing them up in small pieces before adding boiling water will enhance the wintergreen flavor. The little evergreen plant of the boreal forests also bears small red berries with the same wintergreen taste, providing a year-round wilderness treat for the hungry forager. Another tea of the North Country is known as Hudson Bay tea or simply Labrador tea. This member of the heath family has spicy evergreen leaves that can also be gathered and enjoyed throughout the year.

There is a warehouse of exotic tastes to be found throughout the state of Minnesota. I hope this chapter has inspired the reader to partake. Bon Appetit!

Wintergreen berries are a tasty winter treat.

5

The Farm

Once again my husband's and my mutual love for the out of doors resulted in the purchase of a piece of property where we could create and enhance habitat for wildlife. We had searched for several years in central Minnesota before we found a unique area south of Glenwood within the 220-mile glacial ridge. Formed more than 10,000 years ago, receding glaciers had carved out area lakes in this region, and the surrounding land was sculpted into rolling morainic hills. This feature attracted us to a piece of property that not only contained a distinct glacial formation known as a kame, but also oak and basswood woodlands, abundant cattail marshes, natural springs creating small streams, and several ponds near Gilchrist Lake. Open fields containing native grasses, such as big and little bluestem, and wildflowers indigenous to the prairie that I had only seen in wildflower books convinced us that we need look no further.

The title to the property revealed that the 157 acres had been homesteaded and registered by a Mary Mattson in 1902 for a fee of $3.93. Now it was an abandoned and badly vandalized farm, but this didn't lessen our enthusiasm. On a beautiful October afternoon in 1973, we signed the purchase agreement. Afterwards in the glow of the setting sun we walked our property, "the Farm" and witnessed the staging of thousands of migrating monarch butterflies. Clinging to the branches of a huge, old cottonwood tree, they slowly flexed their brilliant orange-and-black wings open and closed—like time-lapse photography of exotic flowers bursting into bloom.

With the idyllic land of the Farm came the vast job of concentrating mountains of trash in the immediate homesite area and dismantling the barn, chicken coop, and five other badly deteriorated buildings. Throughout the decades, previous landowners had pastured assorted livestock on the property, and numerous fields had been sectioned off from one another with miles of barbed and pig wire. This, too, was dismantled. Since cattle were still on the property for the remainder of the year, we elected to "camp" in the kitchen of the decrepit house along with the sparrows and probably dozens of mice. For this nature lover, scampering mice and sparrows flying through the kitchen were not problems. But,

The stalwart silo is the lone reminder of a once successful dairy farm.

curious cows presented a dilemma early one morning as I walked our pregnant collie. I guess they thought she was a new calf in the meadow and came galloping toward us to greet the newcomer. Fearing for her safety and that of her unborn pups, I quickly got the dog in the car and attempted to shoo the cows away. When that failed, this city gal jumped in the driver's seat. Immediately, the pestering bovines surrounded the car and then began chewing on prominent features starting with the headlights. Honking the horn backed them off briefly, but they returned with more determination to sample the license plates. If horn honking didn't phase the placid but persistent cows, it was a major irritation to my archer husband off in the nearby woodlands. Imagine his surprise when he came upon a circle of cows around our red Volkswagon going forward and back with the horn tooting non-stop!

After a year of clean up and salvaging some of the timbers from the farm house, we had amassed the makings for a gigantic bonfire. It wasn't until twenty degrees below zero in mid-January that we enjoyed the warmth from that bonfire while surviving our first and last winter camping trip. The following spring we hired a skilled bulldozer operator to bury the trash and fill in foundations and landscaping where necessary.

Meanwhile, we had moved our campsite to the woods and began to concentrate on our original intent of wildlife management. We consulted the Department of Natural Resources area wildlife manager for advise and, for starters, ditch plugs were suggested for areas that had once held water but had been drained for cropland. Existing ponds, which were undergoing natural succession, needed to be revitalized and, where possible, expanded. We hoped to create a doughnut pond (a water impoundment with a small island in the middle) for waterfowl and have potholes blasted in the marsh for nesting sites.

Through our contact with the Department of Forestry, we embarked on a long-term agreement (LTA) with the Agricultural Stabilization and Conservation Service that involved planting thousands of trees and shrubs for wildlife. Because the property was not only unique structurally, the diversity of soil types allowed us to plant a wide mixture of trees. The species ranged from red and white pine, jackpine, several species of spruce, hybrid poplars, black walnuts, and butternuts. Most fruitful of the shrubs planted for wildlife included buffaloberry and honeysuckle, both of which are especially enjoyed by cedar waxwings and bluebirds.

The LTA also called for culling old and dying trees from eighty acres of existing woodlands. This is when I became the proud owner/operator of a chainsaw. At first I was convinced that these noisy, smelly, gasoline engines were only testosterone friendly and definitely anti-feminine, but reluctantly the saw and I became a functioning unit. As weekend time permitted, and with dueling chainsaws, we culled the mixed timber consisting of bur oak, green ash, basswood, elm, boxelder, and ironwood from the woodlands. Quickly, we amassed huge woodpiles for fuel for the fireplace and fashioned magnificent brush piles for wildlife from the tree limbs.

After erecting several Tom Tubbs plastic wood-duck houses, we began constructing our own wooden design and placed them in preferred habitat. Starting in 1975, six bluebird houses were built each year until our trail numbered seventy-five nest boxes. What a delight it was when we had our first nesting pair of bluebirds. Tree swallows with iridescent greenish-black tuxedo-like plumage, quickly accepted our designs, as did house wrens and rarely, a black-capped chickadee or two.

Through our tree-planting project, we met Palmer Arness, now a dear friend, who offered sage advice, complete with a Norwegian accent and wit. Not only did he drive the tractor pulling the planter upon which we sat while planting thousands of trees, he also planted our five-acre wildlife corn food plot each year. His diverse skill and interests also licensed him as one

of three qualified individuals in the state to use dyna-
mite for excavation purposes. Not only was he known
to blast a beaver dam or two that threatened both crop
and pasture, but he worked closely with the Department
of Natural Resources, as well, for expanding open water
in marshes for waterfowl. With this knowledge and
expertise, he blasted seven potholes in our marsh, and
twenty years later they still remain open.

For five years we camped, mostly in the woods,
but occasionally in the open fields. Each site offering a
variety of wildlife sounds, from the wavering trill of a
screech owl perched outside the tent in the woodlands
to the winnowing of courting snipe when we camped in
the open area. The coyote serenades, territorial barks of
the red fox, and rampaging mice on the tent and
through the forest litter, became our nighttime entertainment. The mornings brought chipmunk scoldings, squirrel chatter, and the liquid notes of various songbirds.
But by 1978, having endured too many extremes of
weather, we started talking about a cabin. And where

*In the forests adjacent to the Farm, the
elegant yellow lady's slipper blooms.*

but on the highest point of the property overlooking the lake could be more perfect? The site facing south lent itself to an earth-bermed, solar-efficient structure that was popular in the late 1970s. Our cabin has been kept rustic without the benefit of running water or electricity. The addition of a wood-burning stove brought warmth as well as ambiance, and propane gas gave us light and a cook stove. Our roofless, naturally ventilated outhouse gave us a window to the world unlike other biffies! Unlike the forests of the north, the open farmlands of central Minnesota reveal skies of unlimited visibility on a clear, moonless night. Why, just the other night on my journey back from the biffy, there was Orion! At last, I've found the elusive, mythological hunter in the south-eastern winter sky. Well, I was pretty sure I saw his three-star-studded belt buckle. Someone's belt buckle. But where was the bow of the hunter and his dog, Sirius, the brightest of the fixed stars, which sits by his master's right foot? Sirius, about the size of earth is actually composed of two stars and one that is charmingly called the Pup. It boggles my mind that our ancient ancestors stood around in the dark playing connect the dots with imaginary lines stretching from star to star, creating eighty-eight arbitrary groupings we call constellations! Perhaps they were imbibing mead when they saw all those mythological characters, inanimate objects and animals in the celestial heavens, but, granted, a constellation such as Orion with stars named Betelgeuse and Rigel is intriguing. The same velvet sky, studded with an incomparable number of stars, is the stage for the aurora borealis as well. And here too, without city lights, the display can be dazzling, and one always has a front-row seat at our intentionally roofless outhouse.

The Farm has given us many special memories, photographic opportunities, the joy of wildflowers, and memorable visual moments of wildlife in a natural setting. Several of the scenes include the curious meeting of a deer and rooster pheasant, cautiously approaching each other until they touched nose to beak! Another time, a very tolerant skunk became the play object of three yearling deer. Nearly rolling the skunk, they cavorted around it and nosed it inquisitively and surprisingly, without apparent repercussion. I have fond recollections of October gatherings of several bluebird families on the patio, putting in an appearance before departing for their wintering grounds. During this time, both adults and young peeked in the windows and lingered just long enough so that I might take notice. The returning spring flocks of hundreds of tree swallows resplendent as they perched on last year's field wildflowers, radiating metallic blue-green in the early morning light.

Monitoring nest boxes on the bluebird trail is always a treat. Walking from birdhouse to birdhouse brings the thrill of the unexpected, such as watching a pair of fawns frolicking like playful kittens or startling a magnificent buck in velvet. Once I encountered a mother skunk with her carbon copy youngsters following behind in single file, and I once came upon the charming scene of a mother raccoon nursing her two week-old cubs in a basswood den tree. The height of the den opening allowing me access to the cubs after mama raccoon departed, to rub their little fuzzy heads while listening to them half purr, half growl in response.

Where we have not planted trees, the land has been allowed to return to its original state. As a result, numerous green ash and oak trees with occasional juniper grow where it was once cultivated or grazed. Willows, osier dogwood, sumac, and snowberry have returned, as well numerous wildflowers in the native prairie areas. Little and big bluestem grasses continue to increase. More trees and shrubs have created more nesting sites and resulted in more birds. The addition of bluebird nest boxes has resulted in bluebirds being the most commonly seen bird during our spring through early fall visits. The thousands of trees that were spared in a spring fire of 1987 continue to flourish, and it is with some pride that all this will be our legacy.

It is our hope that this special piece of acreage will always be a haven for wildlife and, ultimately, when given to the Department of Natural Resources for the continuation of management it will be enjoyed by future generations. For now, it continues to be a source of enjoyment and our weekend wilderness retreat from the maddening pace of the five-day work week in the city.

6

The Bluebird Trail

If the warble of the first bluebird
does not thrill you, know that the
morning and spring of your life
are past.   - Thoreau

Nearly twenty years have elapsed since we
purchased the property we call "The Farm," and, of the
original buildings, only the stalwart silo remains. But we
do produce a "crop" on this non-working farm. By
erecting over seventy-five bluebird houses my husband
has built through the years, we've helped produce
numerous bluebirds, and, until quite recently, these little
blue gems were threatened with extinction. The silo
stands as a reminder of a once thriving dairy farm, and,
as I peer into the coolness of its interior, the floor is ver-
dant with dainty ferns. I notice that once again, an eastern phoebe has attached her cup-shaped nest of mud
and grasses to the south side. Lined with moss and hair,
the nest contains five white eggs. I quickly retreat and
commence my walk along the bluebird trail.

With a clipboard containing a report form, I
record the number of eggs, young, and species from
each nest box. This information will be compiled at the

Adult bluebird perched on a branch watching for insects.

end of the nesting season and submitted to the Bluebird Recovery Program, Audubon Chapter. Two very special people, Minnesota's own Dick and Vi Peterson, have been instrumental in stimulating interest of hundreds of "bluebirders" to adopt their bluebird house design. The "Peterson Bluebird House" can be seen along many bluebird trails, ours included. Ideally, the houses should be placed at least three hundred yards apart, and, through data collected from fellow bluebirders, it has been generally concluded that the preferred direction for nest box openings is east or north. And if they can be placed facing a nearby tree, you will have the "Ritz" location for bluebirds. Although the tree is not necessary, it is ideal landing site for fledglings on their first fluttering attempt to fly.

The establishment of these bluebird trails has brought the bluebird back from the edge of extinction. They were second on the 1980 "Blue List" for a species in a deteriorating situation and a step away from the Endangered Species list. The bluebirds downward spiral began when farmers replaced wooden fence posts with steel, thus eliminating a favored nest site. Add the disappearance of hedgerows and the cutting of dead trees for firewood (as well as for aesthetics), and few nest sites were left for the bluebird. Throw in epidemic numbers of aggressive starlings and English sparrows competing for what few tree cavities existed, and the docile bluebird was quickly and systematically losing out.

My route begins with the sight of an orange glow of the elegant blossoms of wood lilies amongst the emerald green grasses. After this momentary distraction, the soft, sweet, thrush-like warble of *Sialia sialis*, the eastern bluebird is heard from a nearby tree. As I approach the first nest box, a flash of cobalt blue exits quickly. Inspection of the nest reveals four sky-blue eggs, and I rapidly note this on my report form so the female bluebird can return to her clutch. Infrequently, bluebirds do lay white eggs, but nest construction of fine grasses neatly interwoven, readily identifies the species as bluebird. One cool, late spring, a bluebird selected a nest box near a recent deer kill and wove the white belly hair of the dead deer in amongst the grasses of its nest. Having never found hair of any kind in a bluebirds nest in twenty plus years of monitoring nest-boxes, I had to wonder if the birds knowingly selected the hollow deer hair, which traps air, to augment the warmth of the nest.

Quickly, I close the nest box door and move on to the next. Box number two reveals a tree swallow sitting upon one of the most luxurious nests in the bird world! Her nest is lined with layers of silky soft feathers, and I'm envious of the deluxe feather bed. White feathers are highly sought after, and, by waving a single feather above my head, I can attract up to a dozen competitors for the prize. Once the feather has been plucked from my fingers, the game begins as the feather is dropped and picked up by another bird. Quickly, the prize is stolen, and the game goes on until the victor can shove it into its nest box. A recent study implies that by using more feathers for lining the nest, tree swallows produce young that are more robust and quicker to fledge than their neighbors who lack the warm comfort of many feathers. Sheep fleece has been used as an alternative and, on one occasion, stuffed in so thickly, it nearly suffocated the young. Even white, discarded hair combed from our Persian cat has been offered and accepted as nest lining material by tree swallows.

Gently, I stroke the female tree swallow's velvety, metallic blue-green back and mumble my excuse for the rude intrusion. Reluctantly she moves near the rim of the nest, and I count seven snow-white eggs. This too, will be noted on the form attached to my clipboard. Another nearby nestbox also contains seven white eggs, but these are speckled with brown and nearly half the size of the tree swallow's. Immediately I know this is the nest of a black-capped chickadee because the nesting material is almost exclusively moss except for the soft rabbit-fur lining! Actually, before I checked the house I suspected a chickadee was in residence when its nearby mate gave a distinct chickadee call unlike the spring courting song. Tempted

Sometimes chickadees will nest in PVC nestboxes. Already miniature copies of their parents, these seven little chickadees in the opened PVC nestbox are ready to fledge.

to anthropomorphize the call, I thought the cadence fit the words: "Here she comes; here she comes, again." Indeed, it is I, the clipboard-toting lady sporting a tattered and faded green hat and, of course, the ever-present camera dangling from my neck. Chickadees invariably sit tight on the nest, emerging at the last split second to escape harm and, by doing so, nearly colliding with the inspector's forehead! As I continue my semimonthly monitoring, I inhale deeply, detecting the essence of a blooming Russian olive tree wafting on the gentle wind. My inspection of the next local abode is met with angry parents dive bombing me as I make note of six gaping mouths demanding dinner. Tree swallows sometimes develop an "attitude," and rightfully so, if they have survived an attempted raid. As I quickly leave this frenetic family, I see the bicolored plant in shades of yellow and orange called "butter and eggs" that pioneers once planted in their gardens. It is blooming so profusely I can't resist picking several to start my "trail bouquet" of wildflowers.

My trek to the fifth house alarms a white-tailed deer, which gracefully exits by bounding through the yellow woodland sunflowers. Deer are frequently

A late summer nesting produces only three bluebirds in this nestbox.

encountered along the bluebird trail, and it's usually a startling experience for both parties. On a rare occasion, a fawn may be encountered—left lying in dappled sunlight at the forest edge by its mother. So immobilized are young fawns that once I nearly stepped on a newborn one curled in a tight ball, but, with the sound of the lens cap removal, the youngster found its legs and eluded the photographer. Meanwhile, the occupants of this house seems to have flunked basic nest-building class while they excelled in music. The clear musical notes of a house wren come from a nearby tree as I attempt to get an egg count in the disarray of a multitude of small twigs. There, jammed in one corner, order is restored where a tiny grass nest has been constructed and contains two small pinkish-tan eggs splotched with rust.

A monarch butterfly drifting lazily on the breeze escorts me to my next stop. More notes to jot down, and then I walk through a sea of waist high, yellow sweet clover. Ah, another olfactory delight! Its vanilla-like aroma permeates the air, and, I am told, when it dries, the fragrance is intensified. As I approach a wooded glade, the chipmunks are engrossed in some kind of a vocal dispute and seem not to notice me. A Baltimore oriole flies overhead to the old boxelder tree that once again will support the fibrous sack-like nest partially woven from silky milkweed fibers. At that moment I recalled an earlier territorial dispute that took place between two male orioles decked out in their finest breeding plumage. While petals from the fragrant wild plum flew like snowflakes in all directions, the two battled over invisible boundary lines. Now, during the nesting season, blossoming sweet rocket carpets the woodland in waves of pinkish-lavender. The fragrance permeates the air and attracts an assortment of butterflies and even a day-flying moth known as a hummingbird moth. With a fuzzy yellow body and nearly clear wings that beat constantly, it looks like a giant bumblebee.

Proceeding on the trail, I brush past a spruce tree, and a mourning dove cartwheels off a branch, impressively feigning a broken wing as it attempts to lure me away from her two downy chicks tucked into a flimsy nest of small twigs. Crossing the meadow where multiple wildflowers will be picked to complete my bouquet of many colors, I see the small, white blossom heads of sweet-scented northern bedstraw, which will accent the more showy blossoms. Northern bedstraw foliage was once prized as a "filler" for mattress stuffing.

As I continue down the trail, I hear the metallic bubbly notes of a bob-o-link before I spy the spiffy, reversed tuxedo colors of the male, who is embellished with a cape of gold. The next nestbox nest is empty, except for a few old snail shells brought in by parent birds, presumably as a source of calcium or grit.

How rewarding it is to walk the bluebird trail and enjoy Nature's beauty. But, it is part of her scheme that there will be villains in this idyllic setting. There are predators that climb, slither, jump and fly which prey on eggs, young, and even adults in nest boxes. Through unique box designs, many attempted raids are thwarted; baffles or deterring obstacles have been used as well, but for us the most success has been achieved by placing nest boxes on greased, metal fence poles. Among some of the more common predators are mice, chipmunks, squirrels, raccoons, feral cats, occasional bull snakes, and, rarely, opportunistic raptors. Unfortunately, house wrens are becoming a serious threat to bluebirds by usurping nest boxes as well as destroying their eggs. Starlings and English sparrows are the most competitive for nest boxes, and they, too, destroy eggs as well as nestlings.

A slick of grease on the pole holding a bluebird house can reduce predation by a number of animals with a taste for eggs and young birds.

Parasites also create problems for the bluebird, most notably blowfly larva that migrate up from the bottom of the nest box where they hatched from eggs laid by the adult fly. By attaching themselves and sucking blood, they can weaken young fledglings to such an extent that sometimes they cannot recover. Fortunately help in the form of a product called Flies Away II, containing ten percent pyrethrin, a natural insecticide, can be sprayed in the bottom of the box (underneath the nest) to kill the larva and is not harmful to the young birds. Monitoring the bluebird trail at least biweekly can alleviate some of the problems inevitably encountered. Purple Martins, the largest of the swallow family, on the other hand, take their own environmentally friendly approach to insect control by collecting fresh green leaves and stuffing them in the nest. When this green matter is left to decay inside nest compartments, it emits hydrocyanide gas to kill parasites.

Occasionally, minor maintenance may be needed on the birdhouses while doing routine surveys, such as tightening a screw, replacing the closure nail, and evicting summer "squatters" ranging from wasps to frogs to an occasional chipmunk. And one must have some rudimentary skill in building a grass nest! Yup, that's right! As odd as it sounds, grass nests do work in rare emergency situations, such as replacing either a nest damp from a torrential rainfall or one badly infested with blowfly larvae. One pretty summer day my handiwork apparently passed inspection when I had to reconstruct a tree swallow nest. During a survey, I opened a nestbox and found a nest in a slight state of disarray with a odorous, partially desiccated tree swallow pushed off to one side. Finding a dead bird in a house often indicates a raid, and the eggs usually have been broken or abandoned.

Wood lily encountered on the bluebird trail.

Sadly, I removed the dead bird and pulled the nest out slightly to get an egg count. It fell apart in my hand. I was even more disheartened when I felt the eggs. They were "incubation" warm. If I left the situation as it was, the chances of the parent bird reclaiming the nest were slim. Glancing around, I spied a single tree swallow circling high overhead. I assumed it was perhaps the mate, possibly the male who took over incubation when its mate had died.

Uncharacteristically, the nest was about eighty percent feathers and contained a very limited grass supporting base. There was no way I could return the nest for satisfactory incubation. So, while holding a bunch of feathers and eggs in one hand, I reached down, grabbed several handfuls of fine, dry grass with the other hand, stuffing several wads of it in the nestbox and forming a depression. Then, taking the fluffy white feathers one at a time, I laid them down in an overlapping fashion, forming a cozy cup. Satisfied that I had made a pretty darn good nest, I quickly placed the seven eggs in their newly designed quarters. No sooner had I closed the nestbox and moved a distance away, than the lone tree swallow swooped down, alighted at the entrance and immediately disappeared inside the birdhouse to continue incubation. The apparent acceptance made my day!

For many years, my husband has built six additional bluebirds houses during the winter, and these were put up for new customers returning in March from their southern winter residences to our 160 acres. At the end of the year, in spite of some losses, the statistics reveal success for another year, and we get a feeling of pride in knowing we gave Nature a hand by providing nestboxes for these delightful inhabitants of our environment. In Minnesota alone, data collected for 1994 revealed 9,459 bluebirds fledged from 2,403 broods. The Minnesota chapter also compiles information from states coast to coast, border to border as well as from Canada. The western bluebird and mountain bluebird are also cavity nesters and readily adopt nestboxes where Nature once provided them naturally. This combined effort of tabulation resulted in a grand total of 16,274 bluebirds fledged in 1994.

To help these birds that "carry the sky on their back" as Thoreau described them, contact the Bluebird Recovery Program or state Department of Natural Resources.

7

Precocial Babes and Chukar Chicks

They came to us not by choice, but rather by mishap. A brush cutter nearly brought the hen pheasant's demise as she reluctantly left her nest containing thirteen olive-tan, spherical eggs. Had we not experienced previous desertions of nests under somewhat less traumatic circumstances, we would have optimistically assumed she would return after we vacated the area. Only a month previous, our dog had caused a hen to desert her nest of seventeen eggs, and we soon learned that unlike ducks, a pheasant rarely returns once she has been "pushed off" her nest.

Precocial, as opposed to altricial birds, are chicken-like birds. When they hatch, the babies are covered with down, their eyes are open, and, within minutes, they can stand, walk, and most begin searching for food. Pheasants, partridges, quail, turkeys, waterfowl, and even killdeers are all precocial birds. These birds remain in the nest only a few hours, a day at most, and are nearly independent of their parents.

My husband and I share a love for the out of doors and its creatures and felt that, with this second disruption of a nesting hen, we were obliged to give Mother Nature a hand. Even though we knew at the time the hen deserted the nest that she would probably

53

renest, laying fewer eggs, we just couldn't leave the eggs exposed to predators or even worse, let them die. We contacted our area wildlife manager, who helped us obtain permission from the Department of Natural Resources to brood and raise pheasants for release. We had several books about incubating and brooding of gallinaceous birds and quickly adapted a small cooler as an incubator. Maintaining the temperature of ninety-eight to 100 degrees and rotating the eggs three times daily was no problem until we had to leave town after the seventh day of incubation. While most people look for child, plant or pet sitters during their absence, we found ourselves looking for egg sitters! A young couple readily took our wards and dutifully turned the eggs. When we returned to claim our charges, the couple excitedly told us they could hear peeping from within the eggs as well as tapping from beak teeth, which enable chicks to crack the egg open before hatching.

The following day when we arrived home after work, we heard loud peeping emanating from the cooler. Sure enough, when we peered in, there were eleven balls of straw yellow and tan fluff staring back at us in wide-eyed wonder. The innocence and utter helplessness of such tiny creatures melted our hearts. Suddenly we realized we were responsible for these quizzical charmers that seemed to say: "Feed me, I'm yours." After momentary panic, I recalled that as precocial birds they would feed themselves with minimal encouragement. When we sprinkled game bird feed on the plain brown paper lining the cooler, they went by the book, thank heavens! They immediately began pecking at the feed. And by dipping each of their beaks into a small fount of water, they drank!

Quickly, out of necessity, a brooder was made from a large cardboard box and fitted with an infrared lamp to supply necessary warmth. It was a delight to see our balls of fluff flourish. By the end of the second week they were already darting after and inhaling the occasional unfortunate insect that landed in their cage in the garage. We were surprised how much they resembled other young animals in their sleep patterns. Like small puppies, they "crashed" for their naps in a belly flop under the infrared lamp with their stubby wings splayed like leaves that had fluttered to the ground. The third week brought substantial growth and feathering. Instead of jumping straight up in the air like miniature pole-vaulters as they had previously, they flew short grasshopper jumps. By the fourth week, they were flying to the top of the brooder box and becoming increasingly wary.

When we moved them from the protection of the garage down to the marsh at the end of the fifth week, I felt like a nervous mother when youngsters go to camp for the first time. I checked frequently to see how they were adjusting, and that night, when storms were predicted, they were tucked in with a tarp. Next morning at first light, I was pleased to see everyone bright eyed and perky. They had survived the first night in their new environment without incident, and we agreed that with one more night of adjustment and weather stabilization, they would be set free.

The day of release was a glorious summer day. I sat poised with the camera while my husband opened the cage. With only a moment of hesitation, our first fledgling flew out and soared across the pond! The others followed quickly and with the same agility. Soon, we heard the calling of the most robust rooster chick as he tried to locate his siblings. Quickly an answering "peep" was heard. Then another and another until their voices seemed to blend during the next hour, giving me hope they would find each other and remain as a group, enhancing their chance of survival.

As delightful as it is to raise pheasants or waterfowl whose nests have been deserted by the hen or for that matter, chicks obtained from local feed-and-seed stores, it is equally discouraging after release to know that these birds lack the survival "smarts" the hen would have instilled in them. We can only hope that several close calls with predators will educate the young birds and trigger their instinctual wariness.

Chukar Chicks

We didn't intend to tame them! Those clown-faced partridges—native to Eurasia and introduced to the Western United States in the late 1940s—endeared themselves and nearly became "family."

In early June, we purchased one dozen chukars at the feed-and-seed store. As with other gallinaceous birds, these three-week-old chicks were secured in a cage and given access to an ultraviolet light enclosure to maintain their body temperature of approximately ninety-five degrees. Quickly, the young birds flourished on the wild bird maintenance concoction and after several months, they were ready to be released. So, on a beautiful Saturday morning we swung open the pen door and allowed the birds to discover the opening. Excitedly, they dispersed in every direction, and several flew across our pond, crash landing into cattails. But by late afternoon, the troops had reassembled in our front yard, calling to one another like a reunion of long lost friends. Several days later the group split in half, and six camped on the patio. To augment their foraging, we left a feeder with flight maintenance feed available to the birds. As they became more successful at locating their own food, we eventually could stop supplying the commerical feed. But they became addicted to sunflower seeds found not only at the base of birdfeeders, but in the bird feeders! Perched on top of the feeder and looking like condors in contrast to the smaller birds, they began chasing away blackbirds. And if taking control of the birdfeeder wasn't enough, they created potholes in our gravel driveway and lawn as they took multiple dust baths seemingly whenever the urge struck.

Then there was the matter of camping out on the roof and conducting foot races from one end to the other. Although as adults they weigh only twenty-five ounces, our evening meals in the dining room often had

the ambiance of a herd of rampaging miniature ele-
phants above our heads. After the marathons, they
pecked the gravel out of the shingles, convincing my
husband that they'd be better served on a platter.

There are those who hold the belief that Nature
is cruel; where a released pen-reared bird is concerned,
this is especially true. We found the chukars to be quite
tame and nearly indifferent to our dogs and cat. So
docile were these birds that we had to play traffic cop
in the mornings before going to work. With flashlight in
hand, they were rounded up and ushered to the side of
the road so we could back the car out of the driveway.
Sometimes a gentle nudge with the tip of my shoe was
necessary to convince them to move. After one stormy
evening, two of the chukars disappeared, and, several
weeks later after an equally stormy night, two more disappeared. That left only one very lonely bird. It was sad
to see the single bird sitting on a stump, looking down
the vacant road for its buddies. Its repeated calls at sundown to assemble went unanswered, and each evening
as the great horned owls screamed their fright calls, I
hoped the lonesome bird was hunkered down in a safe
haven for the night. But death does not only come on
the apparitional wings of the night hunter. On the
ground, a feral cat, a fox, weasel, or mink could easily
snatch one of these docile birds.

The next evening there were two chukars
beneath the bird feeder eating their favorite sunflower
seeds! Apparently the nighttime attack had scattered the
birds, and the single bird's call united the two.
Throughout the day, these two became nearly insepara-
ble. In the evening, they flew to the roof and disappeared for the night, but, as the week progressed, they
rarely got up together in the morning. Apparently one of
them was a late riser and opted to rendezvous at the
birdfeeder around noon.

They exhibited an amusing behavior that would
occur without logical provocation. Suddenly they would
scurry about like Mad Hatters, darting this way and that

with a stooped posture and wings held slightly aloft. Perhaps a prelude to establishing territories? Perhaps photoperiodism at this time of the year had sent confusing signals to these youngsters as they performed their mock dominance dance for courtship.

As winter progressed, our twosome again became one. Every other evening, the lone chukar appeared a half-hour before sundown. Fluffed out against the cold, its quadrupled size took on the rounded shape of a volleyball while it patiently waited on the patio for a handout. After enjoying a dish of sunflower seeds, it would pace back and forth in front of the patio doors, pecking on the glass. I often interpreted this as an attempt to come inside, but the lone chukar remained wild and eluded any attempt of capture. In spite of this, it apparently became an easy target for an over wintering red-tailed hawk or one of our resident great horned owls. The chukar routinely headed for a secret roosting place overnight, but, sadly, the day before Christmas, the lone survivor fell to a predator and all that remained were several tail feathers near the driveway.

Without capturing and caging the lone chukar for the remainder of the winter, it was doubtful it could have survived Minnesota's coldest months. The native habitat for these birds is the foothill country of Nepal's Himalayan Mountains where the climate bears a similarity to our own Rocky Mountains region. Transplanting these birds to the Midwest had failed twice before the attempt to establish a flock finally took hold in Nevada in 1935. After twelve years, they had adapted so well that unlimited hunting was permitted. They continue to flourish in the western United States, but Minnesota's humid summers and cold winters are hostile to these birds of arid altitudes. In spite of this, local feed and seed stores continue to sell week-old chicks, often to the game farm enthusiasts and occasionally to people like us.

8

Woodland Encounter

I like ruffed grouse; just the scientific name, *Bonasa umbellus,* suggests something unique about this "chicken of the woods." *Umbellus* refers to the ruff, which, depending on the gray or red phase, ranges in color from black to chocolate brown and can be popped out like an umbrella during courtship displays. *Bonasa* is Latin for bison; presumably someone found the drumming of grouse akin to the bellow of buffalo. Of the gallinaceous birds, drumming is unique to ruffed grouse. This means of communication to others of its species is produced when a vacuum created by the rapid lifting of wings from the body allows air to rush into the vacuum, creating the sound. Drumming is most common in the spring but can be heard throughout the year and at any time of day or night.

Photoperiodism stimulates the male grouse to stake out a territory in spring and seek a drumming log. This "log" may be a large stone, a mound, stump, or an actual large old log, preferably with a southern exposure and protective brush or saplings nearby. Drumming starts in March, peaks in April and wanes in May. Most typically, the drummer takes the stage before dawn and by 7:30 A.M. tapers off and may not resume until late afternoon or evening. His performance may be short, only seven seconds, but by repeating the drumming at three to five minute intervals effectively lets the local ladies know of his availability within a half-mile. Starting out slowly as *thump . . . thump . . .* and concluding in a *whirrr,* a grouse's drumming frequently has been compared to an old three-cylinder John Deere tractor starting up. It may even have been our old farm tractor that, one pretty day in mid-May, fired the imagination of a grouse I encountered in our woodlands while collecting firewood.

My husband had started the old farm tractor, attached a utility trailer to the hitch and lumbered down the road into the woods. I followed with a three-wheeled all-terrain vehicle with a small metal trailer. The combination of machines bouncing, snorting and clanking should have scattered all the wildlife in the immedaiate area, but one grouse stood his ground, ready to accept the challenge of a lifetime as our tractor came into view. After our first load of wood had been brought up a steep incline with the three-wheeler, I caught sight of this ruffed grouse peering out at us from the shadows of the forest edge.

The bird was small, probably one of a clutch that had been trimmed to about five or seven at the onset of the previous fall. The average nest contains ten eggs, and, since laying is completed by mid-May, by the time of our intrusion, male grouse certainly had firmly established their territories in the area. This grouse was the rufous or red phase and had a continuous tail band, which suggested a male, but this is not necessarily conclusive. A more reliable index is the length of the two middle tail feathers, which are longer on the male. Another feature unique to the male is that the crest feathers likewise will be longer. Perhaps the most distinctive difference between the sexes is the eye patch known as a comb; males have a salmon to bright orange patch, females have a bluish-gray one. This grouse appeared to have a combination of features, and my limited knowledge of grouse suggested that it was behaving as a territorial male grouse. I had a camera handy and took several pictures. I continued to approach the grouse slowly and eventually got very close. Hoping to assure the grouse that I meant no harm, I started talking to it in a soft, monotone voice. I knelt down to get closer to its level and heard the grouse making sounds I had never heard before. When I arose from my kneeling position the bird followed me throughout the woods, "humming" a tune! I continued to babble my apparently intriguing nonsense, and the grouse just hummed along. I knelt down and searched through the forest litter for a beetle to offer as a friendly gesture, and it rushed at my hand. Much of this activity seemed to be territorial, but in some way it seemed as if the bird behaved like a broody hen, an aberration, or someone's pet grouse.

As I searched for a nest near the bases of trees and logs, my escort putted, purred and hummed its captivating high frequency tune. If momentarily distracted by something beyond the immediate area, the hum increased in intensity, and its crest would rise and fall with the timbre of the serenade. I thought perhaps confirmation of this songster's gender was its preference for the feminine gender—me. It would come to me but fled from my husband. Did it perceive I was an ex-huntress while my husband remained an excellent wing-shooter and preferred his grouse with mushroom sauce? After this encounter however, I learned of several incidents in which a male grouse was a gentleman with women but would attack men or grab their pant legs!

Since I was within the typical one hundred yards of a clearing as well as a woodland path, places a hen would choose for her clutch, I continued to search for a nest. Nearby was a stand of poplar, one of the criteria in nest site selection and, not surprising, also a factor in the male grouse's choice of a drumming log. Everything—good cover, nearness to water and diversity of plant materials—seemed perfect for the location of a nest site.

After a good look around, however, I gave up locating a nest. I thought perhaps I could get some good close-up photographs of this crazy bird that followed me all over the woods! What a ham this feathered creature turned out to be. I would pat a stone and it promptly jumped up and gave me its best profile! The same held true when it posed at the top of a log pile or as it traipsed through the pretty spring foliage of Virginia waterleaf, pausing long enough for yet another photograph.

By now my husband had become intrigued with this odd relationship and suggested that he also document this strange encounter with a photograph. As an enticement for my feathered friend, I looked under several logs to find an irresistible grub, but all I could find was an angleworm. So, worm in hand, I patted the top of a small stump and the grouse dutifully hopped up, and we posed for the camera. Apparently, however, it didn't fancy worms and made this clear by imprinting its beak on my knuckle! As if to educate me further, it did

With a small angleworm in hand, the author has enticed a ruffed grouse onto a stump.

The strangely friendly grouse strikes a pose on a log pile.

a near perfect pirouette off of the stump and devoured a three-leaved basswood seedling.

Even though the woodland was vibrant with spring greenery, I noticed how well this rufous phase grouse blended in with last year's fallen leaves. The other color phase of *B. umbellus* is the gray-phase, and together this unique feature within a species is called dichromatism. It is felt that the gray-phase is considered the bird of the coniferous northern forests, while the red-phase is associated with the central hardwood forest. Presumably the gray blends with the forest pine needle litter and the rufous blends with the leaves of the hard-wood forest. And here in our central Minnesota location where ironwood leaves have a lovely russet coloring and oak a shade lighter, I could appreciate this theory. After a few more photographs, I began to ignore my avian friend, and he began to assume the more typical territorial traits of male grouse. Now he challenged the three-wheeler as my husband attempted to drive it down the hill. Macho Bird, weighing maybe twenty ounces, strutted a zigzag pattern in front of the forward wheel and delayed our wood collecting activity even further. I had read of the bizarre aggressive behavior of male grouse in the spring and knew that they can even viciously attack humans as well as take on automobiles! But *my* grouse had been a charmer and had totally captivated me with its unique personality. Perhaps my experience was not unusual, but I have fond memories of that garrulous grouse that serenaded me with mystical spring music.

9

Eagle Island

It was a special evening, the kind to deposit in a memory bank for withdrawal some cold wintry day. The wind had diminished to a light breeze, the temperature hovered near seventy degrees Fahrenheit, and the sky had just the right amount of fluffy cumulus clouds to guarantee a pretty sundown. As I paddled the canoe over to the island we called Eagle Island, the melancholy laughter of a loon broke the silence. My arrival on the island did not go unnoticed as a sassy red squirrel sounded an alarm. The message was out that an intruder had invaded the island.

I collected my camera gear and began climbing to the precipice of this densely forested island. I walked near the virgin red pine that once again was home to a pair of eagles and noticed the voluminous, windswept branches littering the ground directly beneath the tree. This mountainous tangle of limbs of all sizes attested to the fury of seasonal storms that yearly altered the contour of the huge nest high above. An occasional sooty-gray, natal, downy feather dangled from the understory vegetation, suggesting that the pair of young were in the process of molting. Having observed the eyrie several years before, I always looked forward to the springtime aerial courtship of the bald eagles and their reclamation of this massive nest measuring close to six feet across. It is not unusual for a nest of this dimension to weigh nearly a ton and easily support the weight of a man. The current offspring were probably about four months old and already nearly the size of the adults. But unlike their parents, their mottled, dark-brown plumage would not take on the mature coloration until the age of five. Even though I religiously carried my camera equipment, the thought that I would actually have an opportunity to photograph the eagles never seriously entered my mind as I continued my ascent to the crest of the island. There was no way I could get high enough to look into the nest.

As planned, I took several sundown photos of the panoramic vista of this northern lake. Then, while crouching over my camera bag to switch to a different lens, I heard a mysterious, rather unnerving sound, a kind of "*kak.*" I looked around, searching the depths of the shadows of the island interior and then watched the forest floor for any movement. Nothing. After dismissing the sound, I continued to rummage in the camera bag. A second odd vocalization interrupted the solitude and left me uneasy, actually caused the hair to rise on the back of my neck. I began to think about an escape route. But where? Off the rocky outcropping that rose fifty feet above the lake surface? My imagination began to say: *bear!* Okay, maybe an otter going cross-country, but on a rocky pinnacle in the center of an island? It wouldn't be unreasonable to consider a fisher or pine marten this far north and even though not having the slightest idea what one would sound like, I felt that I could confront a small charging fur ball!

Finally, glancing up, the mystery of the inexplicable sound resolved. Perched on a branch in the towering pine was one of the eaglets, resplendent in the last, rich rays of light. Sitting on the same limb closer to the nest, I saw the second eaglet, and, by its posture, I assumed it to be the subservient sibling. Now that I could associate this odd, low, "*kak*" vocalization with the eaglets, it became a very special moment, almost magical. Having never been so close to an eagle, it was even more of a thrill to see a young eagle just recently out of the nest. Doubling the delight was the discovery that there were two of them. Often there is so much competition between the young that only the strongest juvenile will survive. Occasionally three chalky, white eggs may be laid, but rarely will more than two of the hatchlings survive. This phenomenon is easily understood when one considers that the eggs hatch four to five days apart, thus giving the first out of the shell an obvious size advantage. The youngsters continued their evenly spaced *kak* calls while I reassembled the telephoto lens.

Meanwhile, the adults, soaring on wings spanning over seven feet, circled closer and closer to the island. From a distance they had appeared mere specks in the azure sky, even though they can weigh between eight and sixteen pounds. It is not unusual for them to soar at a height of over a mile, a vantage from which their acute vision allows them to spot fish, which constitutes nearly ninety percent of their diet.

Suddenly I was very aware of my red shirt blazed like a beacon in the setting sun, and I wondered

Recently fledged, an immature bald eagle surveys its world.

if I might be subjected to an aerial attack. Later I would learn that when the young are small and confined to the nest, the adults are, indeed, very protective. But these majestic teenagers had fledged. I hoped the parents would be more tolerant of an admirer's intrusion. After capturing a number of photographs of my cooperative subjects, I quickly dismantled the camera. The deepening shadows of twilight hastened my departure as I descended to the canoe. Gliding across the mirrored surface of the lake, I marveled at my good fortune to have had the opportunity to observe these young, magnificent symbols of freedom, which we, as a nation, adopted in 1782.

Several generations of eagles later, as we look for the return of "our" eagles every late March, I marvel at what a remarkable comeback story has unfolded for the bald eagle population. After thirty years, from a low of fewer than 400 nesting pairs, the population of bald eagles has risen to nearly 4,000 pairs; once threatened with extinction, it has been reclassified as endangered. The category of endangered was cause for optimism. In 1999, with a breeding population of 5,800 pairs, President Clinton announced the proposal to remove this magnificent raptor from the Endangered Species list. Part of the success of the eagle's comeback is thanks to the outlawing the insecticide DDT in 1972. This pesticide had become concentrated in fish, the primary food source of eagles. DDT interfered with calcium metabolism, resulting in thin-shelled eggs that either broke easily, hatched prematurely or, often, were infertile. The bald eagle has further rebounded with the purchase and protection of land with suitable nesting sites and the reintroduction of eagles to areas where they previously had lived. Some of this reintroduction has been through captive breeding efforts or, recently, by the removal of eggs or young from nests located in Minnesota's Chippewa National Forest, which has the largest breeding population in the lower forty-eight states. Within the last few years, these eggs or young have been transplanted successfully to nests within the forests of Tennessee as well as areas of upper New York.

Ironically, with their increase in population, bald eagles are competing with and displacing osprey ("fish hawks"). Also, it concerns some that, in desperation for nesting sites, some eagles, possibly to their detriment, are nesting closer to human habitation than ever before. Typically a territorial range of one acre or more is needed around a nest site where the preferred tree selection is the tallest red or white pine near water and ideally situated at the shallow end of a lake, an advantage for spotting fish. Such is the location for "our" eagles, and we have been fortunate to watch the magnificent adults fly to a pilot tree or snag before alighting on the nest to feed their young. We have watched the young flap, jump and hop madly about in the nest, testing their wings, gaining strength and confidence before becoming airborne. By hovering just above the nest with a fish, the adult entices the hungry young to leave the nest. Once, on a warm and humid summer morning, we had the opportunity to spy on the bathing ritual of an adult eagle at the shoal end of the island. Not unlike a robin, it too stooped and rolled its shoulders into the shallow water several times, sending a shower of water over its back before shaking off a cascading spray of droplets. But unlike most birds and a surprising revelation to us, was the anhinga-like posture the eagle assumed when drying its feathers. Flying to a nearby dead tree, the eagle extended both wings while perching motionless, letting the wind riffle-dry its damp feathers.

For us, our eagles are the harbingers of spring in the North Country. Though when they return to their island, the lake is still frozen, they do have limited open water at the north end of the lake from which to pluck a fish out of the icy waters. Also willing to dine with other scavengers at a deer kill, bald eagles manage to sustain themselves during the lean months before ice out. Once during March as we entered a frozen bay, we saw two adult eagles hunched over a strange looking object. As we viewed the scene with binoculars, we realized the object was a large, upside down turtle; later, closer inspection revealed the hapless reptile to be a footless as well as headless painted turtle. We wondered if the eagles had intimidated an otter at the nearby lakeside opening of a beaver dam, claiming the prize as theirs.

Every March, all we need hear is the cry of the eagles as they circle high above in the azure sky, and we know all is well in the northern coniferous forest. In autumn, we always bid a sad farewell to them, hoping their migration south for the winter will be a safe journey and that the eagles will return as a pair. We feel privileged to be a part of their wilderness and hope the bald eagle will always soar and captivate admirers.

10

Butterfly Behavior

Butterflies are among the most colorful insects in the world, and they, like so many other creatures, are slowly losing their habitat. Some species of butterflies, of course, have already disappeared along with many animal and plant species. It would indeed be a sad world if we lost any more of these gossamer sprites that visit our summer flowers, adding fleeting brilliance or iridescence as they flit through forest and field. Butterflies belong to the order Lepidoptera, a combination of Greek words translating to: "scale wings." These scales, overlapping like fish scales or roof shingles, not only create the color patterns, they help in the aerodynamics of these spectacular flying machines. The butterfly's agility of flight is enhanced by the dual purpose of both sets of wings. The forewings are designed for flight and power. Hindwings steer and glide, helping to create their erratic maneuverability. Recently, it has also been found that glands at the base of some scales on the hindwings produce pheromones to help attract a mate.

There are about 700 species of butterflies in North America. One hundred forty of these reside in Minnesota, seven of which have the ability to hibernate. After sleeping through sub-zero winter temperatures in crevices of trees and amongst forest litter, these hardy butterflies may even emerge on a warm, late winter day, as long as the temperature rises to at least fifty-five degrees Fahrenheit. Butterflies must be able to elevate their body temperature to eighty-one degrees before they can take flight. By positioning their bodies at an angle that maximizes solar gain, they absorb enough heat to "fuel" their lift off even if actual temperatures don't register eighty-one degrees.

These harbingers of spring bring a splash of color to the drab landscape. The most commonly seen wintering over butterfly in the North Country is the mourning cloak. With a wingspan of three inches, the rich mahogany-brown wings are edged with electric blue dots and trimmed with a golden strip to the outer most aspect. Other hibernating members of this Nymphalid family include the angle wings, tortoise shells, red admiral, and painted lady. As members of the brush-footed family, the first of their three pair of legs (all insects have three pairs of legs) are stunted, pulled up against the thorax and covered with bristles, hence "brush-footed."

Butterflies as a whole are unique. They taste with their feet, smell and hear with their antennae, drink nectar through a one-and-one-half-inch soda straw-like proboscis that curls up like a watch spring, and several species migrate to warmer climates for the winter.

The feature of hibernation is a most fascinating phenomenon and is dependent on a number of factors. For a butterfly to survive temperatures as cold as minus forty degrees Fahrenheit, cryoprotectants must be pro-duced. The length of day (photoperiodism) and cooling temperatures stimulate their bodies to produce enzymes and triggers the synthesis. When glycogen is converted to glycerol, it acts as antifreeze by drawing moisture out of the cells. Here the water may freeze, but outside of the cell membrane, preventing the rupture of the cell wall. It is interesting to note that the water droplets freeze into rounded forms rather than sharp crystals, which eliminates damage to the sleeping insect.

No discussion of butterflies would be complete without mentioning the amazing mystery of monarch migration. Millions of these beautiful orange-and-black butterflies, with a wingspan of four inches, migrate by day as well as night, over 1,800 miles at elevations ranging from 1,500 to 7,000 feet. With a cruising speed of only twelve miles an hour, it is not surprising to learn that they utilize thermals and "go with the flow" of weather systems heading south. Several sources have documented the presence of magnetite or magnetic iron oxide in their bodies, leading some to speculate all eastern monarchs migrate by using the earth's magnetic field to find their way to the Michoacan forests of Mexico. Nature has programmed the returning generation, consisting primarily of mated females (only one percent of which will return to the northern states), to live as long as eleven months while their progeny live only three months. These are but a few of the mysteries of monarch migration still unfolding to the scientific community.

The monarch caterpillar feeds exclusively on milkweed, by human standards a very bitter and toxic plant. The larva and adult butterfly are, thereby, rendered toxic to birds. It is this feature that allows the "Batesian" mimicry of the look-alike viceroy butterfly to survive virtually predator free, for once a bird has regurgitated a monarch, it will avoid all large orange-and-black butterflies!

Another adaptation butterflies can exhibit is the ability of several species to camouflage their brightly colored wings by simply closing them, allowing the drab, patterned undersides to blend in with dead leaves; brush-footed butterflies are masters of this disguise. This disappearing act not only belongs to the adult butterfly, but the caterpillars of these same species often not only blend into their surroundings, they adapt to variation in coloration of individual vegetative locales.

Nowhere else in the insect world is the phenomenon of metamorphosis, the transition from egg to adult, more dramatic than in Lepidoptera. The intriguing capability to select the right species of plant upon which to lay its eggs is in part achieved through taste. By scratching the surface of leaves with her feet and, thereby releasing plant chemicals, the female butterfly "tastes" each plant before laying an egg. Eggs are most often laid singly on the undersides of leaves and come in a varying array of forms from conical, spherical or flattened. The length of time from laying to hatching varies, and some eggs may even over winter, but frequently the time period can be as little as three to four days. When the tiny caterpillars hatch, they will first consume their own eggshell before feeding on the host plant. After several weeks of marathon munching and molting its skin four to six times, the caterpillar selects a secluded spot and changes into a chrysalid. As early as several weeks later and through metamorphosis, the adult, an *imago*, will emerge. A striking exception is a northern species, the Canada arctic butterfly, which takes two years to achieve the adult form!

Tiger swallowtails, as the name implies, are large, yellow-and-black-striped butterflies commonly seen throughout most of the United States. It is one of several species that produces two broods per year and, in the case of the tiger swallowtail, the first hatch emerges in May. A trait frequently observed in the males of this species and usually noted in the second generation is that of "clubbing." This ritual often consists of a number of predominantly male tiger swallowtail butterflies congregating on moist sand, probing with their proboscis while concentrating sodium necessary for mating. This is a curious phenomenon to observe, and once I watched as one such butterfly took in so much moisture that it expelled excess water as a droplet off of the tip of the abdomen every ten to fifteen seconds.

Those buttery-yellow, medium-sized butterflies noted in early autumn are the common sulphur butterfly, and they, too, amass in large numbers around puddles. This "puddling phenomenon" is perhaps for the same reason that the swallowtail partakes—to extract minerals from the sand. Uric acid found in carnivore urine or scat is particularly enticing to the white admiral butterfly. When the dung contains blueberry residue, several of these pretty butterflies will dine, nearly oblivious to human observation. Fermented fruit, such as apples or oranges, will likewise attract brush-footed butterflies, especially the angle wings and a group of medium size butterflies known as satyrs.

Most species in the animal kingdom have a need to establish territories, and this is no less important for the diminutive butterfly. Male butterflies become combative in defense of territory when a boundary has been crossed. Not only will they pursue a trespassing butterfly, they will "chase" the family pet, escort a human to the perimeter, or even take off after birds. The intense need to protect their piece of turf is primarily for perching on the edge of an open area where they watch for and court members of the opposite sex.

I witnessed a mysterious event involving a black swallowtail butterfly. I watched one bright spring day as a female black swallowtail, momentarily baffled by the chickenwire fencing, sailed over the top to investigate the barren garden within. The previous summer I had raised carrots, parsnips, and parsley in that section of garden and, not surprisingly, a number of black swallowtail larva as well, since the family to which all three of these plants belongs is the favorite of this species of butterfly. Several times she flew up and down where the rows of carrots had been nearly nine months earlier. Upon not finding parsnips either, she located a potted parsley plant that I had over wintered indoors and had just set out in the garden in a new location. Scratching the surface of a leaflet with her forefeet released the desired chemical scent, telling her this would do nicely. Several eggs were laid before she departed. How did she know the alignment of the rows as well as the number of rows? Did she somehow have a "memory" of where the plants had been? Several other documented

Homegrown on carrot greens, this black swallowtail butterfly emerged from a chrysalis and was set free to alight on the contrasting red geranium.

observations by scientists have shown butterflies can learn to avoid a previous site of capture or to even change its preference for a particular flower for which it has unique adaptations, to that of an unknown variety. It's difficult to comprehend the multiple complexities of such a feather-weight of beauty!

11

Doughnut Dividends

Another ninety-degree day. The drought continued and the sun blazed down on the parched earth. I
had debated whether to stay in the cool comfort of our
farm cabin or go down to the "doughnut" to investigate
the red algae growing on the nearly evaporated surface
water. Over fifteen years before we had created this
impoundment (shallow water reservoir) in the loamy,
naturally depressed area that had been drained for agricultural purposes many years earlier. Shortly after our
acquisition of the Farm, we had contacted the
Department of Natural Resources for advice on improv-
ing the area for wildlife habitat. This consultation resulted in the proposal to create three additional ponds on
the 160-acre parcel. Through a cost-sharing program
available to private land owners, we arranged to have
these three areas "plugged" (the placement of dikes at
the point of earlier drainage) and excavate the "doughnut." Having secured the proper permits from several
agencies, our wildlife manager put us in contact with an
experienced backhoe operator for excavating and con-
touring the doughnut site, now more commonly called a
"dugout." The basin was sculpted to a maximum depth
of three feet, and a dike was constructed at the point of
the previous drainage. The rich soil removed is called

the "spoil," and this was evenly distributed not only on the surrounding periphery, but a thin layer was returned to the basin, forming an organic base that, when covered with water, allowed growth of aquatic vegetation. Hay distributed over the entire area helped with soil stabilization. A mound of soil in the middle of the basin formed the "hole" of the doughnut or an island for a predator-free waterfowl nesting/loafing site. Without any additional help from us, good vegetative habitat quickly grew, and, the following year at the inner periphery of the water's edge, arrowhead quickly took hold. This plant, easily identified by the shape of the leaf is also known as *wapato* or duck potato. The starchy tubers it produces were once a favorite of American Indians, and early settlers soon learned to harvest this tuber during lean periods. The small tubers found at the end of root fibers is a favorite food of muskrats. In the fall, migrating ducks readily consume any free-floating tubers that have bobbed to the surface.

Another marsh plant called bur reed also flourished, perhaps "planted" by migrating ducks as the partially digested seed was deposited along the shoreline. The tall, grass-like leaves and its spiky seed ball also are a delicacy for waterfowl as well as providing cover and nesting sites. The creation of the doughnut has provided nesting cover for several species of ducks, and a pair of Canada geese claimed it one year and produced five goslings before the ducks reclaimed the island once again. Even though the drought of 1988 in central Minnesota had lowered the water level, the doughnut remained an oasis of activity for all forms of wildlife.

When I arrived at the doughnut, there was beauty to be found in a hot afternoon under the unrelenting rays of old Sol in late June. The camera was quickly mounted on a tripod, and, with sweat-soaked eyes, I focused on a dragonfly identified as a brown-spotted yellow-wing. In the sunlight, the clear areas of the wings glistened like transparent topaz. Concentrating on my rather fickle subject, I was surprised to hear an egret abruptly take flight just a few yards away from me, its raucous croaking obviously annoyance at being disturbed while hunting frogs in the shallow water. Suddenly the source of the alarm came into view—a beautiful buck in velvet. But as quickly as he had appeared, he seemed to vanish. Hoping to capture the buck on film, I tried to step quietly over hummocks that ringed the edge of the doughnut. In doing so, I noticed multiple deer beds amongst the tall sedges. Out of the corner of my eye I saw movement on the surface of the algae. With sinuous undulations, a garter snake glided through the combination of green and red algae. The striking contrast begged for a photo, so, with more metallic racket, I adjusted the tripod and snapped several photos.

While looking about and savoring the sweet redolence of milkweed and linden blossoms, a large, orange-and-black butterfly known as a great spangled fritillary alighted on a nearby milkweed blossom. A picture not to be ignored, if only the wind would slow down a knot or two! More adjustments, more noise, but still no sign of the buck I was hoping to catch on film before I left the area. The little black-masked warbler, known as a common yellowthroat, announced its presence from the shade of an osier dogwood thicket with its *witchity . . . witchity . . . witchity* call as I pursued my quarry. Finally, with perfect timing, the buck arose from his bed to investigate the stentorian disturbances taking place in his territory, and I had the camera focused on him as he stared in disbelief. After allowing me my one photograph, he was off in a flash.

I saw an eastern tiger swallowtail butterfly using its proboscis clubbing the moist soil to extract sodium. Sodium along with amino acids is thought to be vital for future progeny. The moist soil also revealed tracks probably made when a killdeer probed the muck looking for small crustaceans. Bluet damselflies of reddish as well as blue hues played tag in the marsh grasses and paused long enough for another photo, representatives of the varied marsh inhabitants. What a visually rewarding afternoon it had been. I was delighted with my decision to endure the heat and discover a myriad of activity at the doughnut, even though by most human comfort standards, this day would have been considered intolerable. Through the seasons and over the years, the scene continually changes at the doughnut, and, along with it, the inhabitants. Muskrats that were occasional visitors, have set up housekeeping on the mini-island and probably help to keep the body of the doughnut open as they forage for aquatic vegetation. Beavers are now the occasional visitors as they seek tender bark from young willows before discarding the stripped branches for dam site re-enforcement in the adjacent wetland flowage created by natural springs. Raccoons hunt frogs and crustaceans in the watery haven while fox and coyote come to the water's edge at sundown for a drink before setting off on their nightly forays. And for four to six weeks in the spring when male leopard frogs are crooning for the ladies, nesting geese keep a watchful eye on the opportunistic mink waiting for the right moment to rush in and raid their nest.

With the impact of grazing cattle no longer a factor in this ecosystem, the adjacent meadows became abundant with wildflowers, attracting an assortment of butterflies and insects. Even the doughnut's surface water is home to several floating plants, two of which blossom. In spring, water crowfoot blooms so profusely with white flowers, it looks as though large snowflakes have blanketed the water surface. The other plant, bladderwort, is carnivorous and produces pretty, yellow snapdragon-like flowers. The plant is so named because of the bladder forming pods among the submerged plume-like leaves. These pods contain a trapdoor triggered by sensitive hairs. When tiny water insects touch the hairs, the door opens and sucks in its victim. The third plant is aquatic duckweed, a one-lobed, free-floating, stemless plant savored by ducks. It is unique in that it stores starch throughout the summer, becoming so

A fritillary butterfly sips nectar from a black-eyed Susan.

A white admiral butterfly probes the rocky soil for mineral-laden moisture.

heavy by autumn it sinks to the bottom of ponds to survive the hardships of winter. In spring, the plant is so light after having depleted its food stores, the little green plant bobs to the surface to repeat the cycle again.

One outer section of the doughnut contains an assortment of willows and osier dogwoods that grew up amongst black walnut trees we planted many years earlier. This change in the landscape has added to the diversity of bird populations due in part to a tiered effect of the shrubbery and trees that created better nesting habitat. Some of these same shrubs provide berries as well as browse for white-tailed deer and rabbits. The berries of the osier dogwood are eagerly sought by songbirds, most notably the catbird and eastern bluebird.

An indirect benefit of willow regrowth has been the proliferation of the "diamond willow," which is not a distinct species but rather a victim of a fungus that can infest any member of the willow family. When a skilled woodcarver's knife has carved and caressed the grain of the wood, beauty emerges, and the diamond pattern becomes a beauty spot instead of a fungal scar where a branch once resided.

Even after more than twenty years, the doughnut rates pretty high on my must-explore list when we arrive for our weekend retreat. Whatever the season, there are always discoveries to be made, mysteries to be investigated, and, we have concluded, it was indeed a good investment for wildlife.

12

Raptor Reminiscences

Several years ago after reading numerous, informative articles about the Gabbert Raptor Center situated on the University of Minnesota's campus in St. Paul, we became members of this unique organization. Upon completing a tour of their facilities and being enlightened through a slide presentation narrated by one of the many volunteers, we became even more committed to the concept of healing and releasing raptors. We began to understood fully the origin of word "raptor" and how important these aerial predators are in our diminishing ecosystem. The term is derived from the Latin *rapere*, meaning to seize or grasp. With predatory birds such as raptors, this must be done with precision in order to survive. Wanting to become more involved, we sponsored two rescued raptors and followed their progress recuperating from injuries. Having attended one of the biannual releases of such raptors, I had the fortune of being selected to release one of these magnificent birds of prey back into the wild.

The following is an account of two special, diminutive owls and a red-tailed hawk, all of which were treated at the Gabbert Raptor Center for assorted maladies.

Odie, the barred owl, is one of several raptors representing the "Educational Birds" at the Gabbert Raptor Center.

Spirit

A warm autumn day, mid-October, and the last of the luminous yellow birch leaves fluttered to the ground—it was time for the annual yard clean up, and the empty child's wading pool became a receptacle for twigs and branches before leaf raking began in earnest. Around twelve o'clock noon as the homeowner of this rural setting drove up the driveway, she glanced at the backyard and saw a gray lump sitting on the rim of the pool. The hunched diminutive size and ear tufts momentarily suggested a small kitten. But as the "lump" hopped down and hobbled to the woodpile, it became obvious that this was an injured screech owl.

Six months previous, this small raptor's eyes had opened to a fascinating world awaiting exploration while sharing a nest with as many as four brothers and sisters. Accommodations were sparse; no additional nesting material was provided when the five white, unmarked and nearly round eggs were laid in late

March in a hollow of a tree five to fifty feet high. After adult plumage started to replace the downy coat of white fluff, the color phase began to emerge in shades of grey. Quickly the nestlings flourished on a high-protein diet ranging from insects, frogs, and minnows to small birds and rodents.

Shortly after a month from hatching, the young fledged and, with parental guidance, learned survival skills for the nocturnal world. But all the teachings of an adult could not prepare one young owl for what fate had in store. Nature is sometimes cruel and full of perils for even an experienced adult owl. Most devastating to raptors of all kinds is the invention of humans. This owl became a victim, a collision casualty of unknown origin. But destiny was on its side when the concerned citizen found it and conferred with the local Humane Society and the DNR. The injured owl was placed in a box and taken to the Gabbert Raptor Center. This organization, co-founded in 1972 by doctors Gary Duke and Pat Redig, was created for the purpose of treating and reha-

Another raptor, this one an immature red-tailed hawk.

bilitating injured raptors (hawks, owls, falcons, and eagles) and then returning them to the wild. So successful has this program been that, in 1992, they anticipated admitting their 7,000th patient. Nearly half of the birds brought to the clinic are successfully treated and released to the wild. If not too a long a period has elapsed since injury, the birds may be returned to the area in which they were found.

Upon arriving at the Raptor Center, the injured screech owl was registered as R-481. Quickly, skilled hands assessed the extent of the injuries. Not only was the owl in shock, listless and non-aggressive, it also had mild head and eye trauma and a broken wing. Its weight of 150 grams (normal 180) indicated this was a female. Because of partial dehydration, fluids were

given as well as antibiotics, and, with hand feeding for two days, the patient was stabilized for surgery. On day three, surgery was performed on the wing, and a pin was inserted. The wing was then taped to the body. Afterwards, the owl was placed in a small convalescent cage where bandages were changed twice a week. Twelve days later, the pin was removed. Two weeks later, physical therapy began three times a week; the wing needed to be stretched to improve the range of motion. This was done under anesthesia so as to minimize pain and stress plus it allowed the muscles to stretch more easily. With the dedication of volunteers, extensive flight retraining commenced. After six weeks, an assessment was done to see if the young owl could eventually return to the wild.

During this stage of the owl's rehabilitation, I learned that my donation and request to sponsor a screech owl at the Raptor Center had assigned R-481 to me. Several days later the Adoption Certificate, a letter of introduction and an artist's likeness of a screech owl, along with a fact sheet for the species, arrived in the mail. And I was elated! The thought that I could make a difference and help one of my favorite species of owl return to the wild thrilled me. I wanted to know everything about my new ward and its kind as well as the rehabilitation program. I selected the name "Spirit" to replace "R-481." I wanted to believe "my girl" would excel in Rehab Flight I-A, that she had the will to gain her freedom and that, once again, she would maneuver through the countryside with the silent apparitional grace characteristic of owls.

However, monitoring her progress via telephone revealed that her test flights demonstrated no further progress; without symmetrical strength in her wings, Spirit would not be able to successfully hunt prey. In other words, my adoptee would not be a candidate for the spring raptor release. Though disappointed and knowing Spirit would spend the rest of her life in captivity, I knew she would be used in educational presentations to enlighten the public about the value of raptors. After fifteen weeks of convalescence and labeled "permanently disabled," Spirit left the Raptor Center January 31 for the Chahinkapa Zoo in Wahpeton, North Dakota. Her journey was first class all the way, from courier service to and from the airport to free airfare compliments of Northwest Airlines.

When I heard a screech owl's quavering trill in the darkness of night, I would think of a little gray "lump" named Spirit, who was given a second chance and perhaps more importantly, became an "educational bird" to help future generations of raptors. She became a favorite of the zookeeper and his family, who looked forward to see her emerge from her nestbox and perch nearby every evening at sundown. But Spirit's life was mysteriously cut short. After only four months in her new home, she was found dead one morning.

Tawny

"What? You want to adopt another owl?" My friends obviously questioned my sanity. When I explained that this new owl also had a broken wing and head injuries, they knew this wildlife enthusiast had gone off the proverbial edge. Upon explaining how this pathetic, feathered ball of fluff was found injured and how it, too, would be rehabilitated through the Raptor Center's program, they wanted to know more.

This owl, like nearly fifty percent of patients admitted to the Raptor Center, was a victim of a collision, most likely with a car. It was discovered sitting alongside County Road 7 on a cold November day near Princeton, Minnesota. The chocolate coloring and facial markings forming distinctive eyebrows to create a "V" down to the bill confirmed it was a very young saw-whet owl. The adults lack this formation and have more striations; often, this juvenile form has been mistaken for a new species. The good samaritan who found the owl put it in a box, which protected the flight feathers and provided a dark, secure confinement creating a calming

Saw-whet owl (above). (Courtesy of the Minnesota Zoo)

A northern harrier, more commonly known as a marsh hawk, consuming a red-winged blackbird.

affect on the bird. Upon arrival at the center, the owl's weight was recorded as a mere 105 grams and the owl was determined to be a female. Because she had food in her stomach and, for the most part, was in pretty good shape, she probably had been discovered quite soon after the injury. X-rays revealed a broken collarbone, but because of the location of the break, surgery was not necessary. Rather, the wing was taped to the body to restrict movement and allowed to heal naturally. Treating the partially detached retina in her left eye was of more concern. This type of injury is not unusual in impact traumas. On the other hand, the formation of a blood clot that could migrate to the brain does occur quite often and would mean the sudden demise of the raptor. The little owl was assigned the identification number of S-616. Her eye was treated with antibiotic and steroid ointment to aid in re-attachment.

In keeping with the successful program of rehabilitation, S-616 was started on physical therapy shortly after her arrival. Initially, the treatment consisted of stretching the wing in order to keep muscles elastic, and soon was given short fluttering exercises. Graduate classes consisted of flight therapy and "live training" over several months. The latter essentially retrains the raptor to hunt and catch prey. During recuperation, S-616 was given dead mice; afterwards, because she was so young, she would have to learn to catch her own live mice in order to be a candidate for release.

I have always had a fondness for owls and wanted to "adopt" a saw-whet owl, not only because of their reported tameness, but also from my own close encounter in the wild with one of these feathered sprites. S-616 was assigned to me. Quickly I renamed her "Tawny" for the ochre coloring on the chest area. Since she was slated for a late spring release, I had time to study her species before she became a memory. Research revealed that her parents probably had begun courting in April. Often, their courtship vocalizations can be heard after 10:00 P.M. emanating from dense forests. This has been described as a rhythmic "beeping," occurring at a rate of 100 to 130 times per minute. Having decided to set up housekeeping, the pair selected either an old woodpecker hole or a natural cavity. Austere accommodations—no lining material cushioned the five or six white eggs in the bottom of the hole. After several weeks incubation, which began when the first egg was laid, the parents became rapacious

hunters of mice and other small rodents to feed their rapidly growing young, which would measure a diminutive seven to eight inches in height when mature.

This little owl gets its name from their infrequent, raspy call that sounds like a saw being sharpened. However, when young saw-whet owls beg their parents for food, it is a spooky whinnying cry. Having large, round, yellow eyes, they appear less stern than other owls and though nocturnal, they can be found dozing during the day in dense conifers and are easily approached. There are accounts of this bird being so docile it can be picked up by hand. But one must respect that it is wild, admired but not touched.

The date of the spring raptor release came and went, and Tawny, although mended, remained behind in a "Padded Cell!" It was explained that a problem, not uncommon to saw-whets, is that their tail feathers are

An American kestrel (top) and a rough-legged hawk (bottom), both educational raptors at the biannual raptor release program of the Gabbert Raptor Center.

battered to such an extent in captivity that they are unable to obtain "lift off." Apparently, when the owl has fully recuperated from its injuries, it becomes so active with the onset of darkness that traditional wire cages take a toll on a confined bird's tail feathers. So, until Tawny grew some satisfactory replacement tail feathers, she would remain a patient.

Having gone through a molt and grown new tail feathers, Tawny was now equipped with a functional rudder that met the approval of the raptor technicians who signed her release form. Nearly ten months after her injury, she was set free.

S-219's Freedom Flight

It is perhaps the relase of S-219, a red-tailed hawk, that I hold the most special of my raptor memories.

In the autumn of 1992, twelve weeks had elapsed since the red-tailed hawk I cradled upside down in my arms had flown in the wild. I had won the chance to set this beautiful bird free after it had fully recovered from a mysterious malady. When it had been declared ready for flight, it was fitted with a leg band, Federal Number 1387-43533. As Dr. Pat Redig read the history of this raptor to a crowd of about 300 onlookers, I hurled it skyward. The young hawk soared magnificently to a distant tree.

Red-tailed hawks are common throughout the United States and are the most common hawk admitted to the clinic. This is a large bird, weighing between two and four pounds with a wingspan of forty-eight centimeters. The young do not achieve the identifying red tail until their second year. This particular species dines almost exclusively on rodents and is a vital link in the well-being of our environment.

What a thrill it was to be privileged to set this raptor free and to know that it had been given a second chance to soar the thermals thanks to the dedicated staff at the Gabbert Raptor Center.

13

Signs of Autumn

As a late summer northwest wind ripples the cat-tails like a wave of an incoming tide, it brings a fore-boding of inevitable cold. Decreasing sunlight hours create a sense of urgency in all living things in the Northern Hemisphere. The signs are there. It is time to prepare for the long winter sleep. Time to shut down the chlorophyll factories, let the wind scatter seeds for next year's flowers, stock the pantry and insulate that winter den. Time for assemblage—bird or butterfly. Warmer climes will soon beckon as temperatures slowly drop and food supplies dwindle.

The subtleties have started to amass silently behind the footfalls of summer. There is a splash of crimson on sumac bushes, flowering goldenrods spread a glow of sunshine across fields, and occasional luminous, yellow leaves punctuate the summer green of poplar trees. Wild asters—in shades of white to dark lavender—entice yellow sulphur butterflies to sample their nectar. Four species of insects, two of which are moths and two are winged insects of another order are already snug in their pulpy, bulbous winter home in the goldenrod stems. Already, chill touches the evening air, sunsets come earlier, geese fly in small "V" formations, and small flocks of ducks, perhaps from the spring

hatch, perfect their landings by repeatedly alighting and taking off from our pond. Like a holiday greeting card, the vermilion leaves of Virginia creeper vines entwine deciduous tree branches, contrasting with still-green leaves. It's only the last week of August, but the cool temperatures foretell the coming of frost. Squirrels of the

In the year 2000, the brilliant orange-and-black monarch became Minnesota's state butterfly. Soon it will begin staging for migration.

Opposite page: Autumn bouquet: wood-land sunflower, great blue lobelia, joe-pye weed, flat-top white aster, red-stalked aster, lythrum, blanket flower, stiff golden-rod and Canada goldenrod.

Mallard secondary wing feather against dry grasses.

boreal forests continually interrupt the solitude as the nutritious, seed-bearing pine cones severed high atop the trees fall to the ground with heavy thuds. When this noisy rain of pine cones hits the cabin roof, the family pet becomes a bit paranoid and scurries for protective cover under the bed. In the deciduous woodlands, a bountiful acorn crop is already dropping, providing mast not only for squirrels and deer, but also for birds, especially woodducks. With a sense of urgency, industrious muskrats build their domed winter homes of cattails and pond muck in the marshes while other mammals hoard winter food supplies and put on extra layers of fat for hibernation. Some, such as woodchucks, put on a layer of super-energy-releasing "brown fat." Without conscience for their gluttony, but with instinct for a need to cache food for the long winter ahead, chipmunks empty every sunflower seed feeder as fast as they are refilled.

The insect world too has picked up the tempo. Katydids and crickets sing more lustily now, hoping for an encore, another night of music before the curtain of frost closes the show. Late summer monarch butterflies are on the wing, preparing for migration to their wintering grounds high in the mountains of Michoican, Mexico. On occasion, the large green darner dragonflies, who likewise are heading south, accompany them. By the end of September, ladybugs will begin to congregate, being stimulated by pheromones signaling the need to hibernate in large groups. In some woodland areas, thousands upon thousands of these red-backed and black-spotted bugs coat every stem, leaf and branch before settling beneath forest litter in a state of dormancy over winter. Soon "woolly bear" caterpillars will scurry across the patio in search of a cozy, secure hibernation retreat. Folklore has it that these fuzzy-coated weather forecasters predict the severity of the coming winter by the width of the orange central band. In reality, each time a woolly bear molts, which can be four or more times in the fall, the width of the orange band varies.

A multitude of wispy, gossamer cobwebs float on the breeze with delicate ghostly grace as spiders begin "ballooning," a term used to describe how young spiders or "spiderlings" spin a thread of silk to sail on a breeze to a new location. Those that aren't floating about are trying to set up housekeeping in the farthest reaches of basements hoping for balmy temperatures in which to over winter. Several species of flies seeking warmth on cool afternoons line up on outdoor screen doors and door casings, waiting to accompany the humans inside. Mist rising above the pond creates an apparitional backdrop for the trisyllabic call of the great horned owl. Restless as well as noisy blackbirds form undulating waves, swarming over the cattails in large flocks. Arctic terns, which spend the winter at the southern tip of South America, have already set migration in motion by the last week of July. Soon other shorebirds follow suit, leaving their northern nesting grounds well before the first of September. Warblers, also early migrants, begin filtering down from the boreal forests. Having donned their drab autumn-colored plumage, the phrase of "confusing fall warblers" makes sense when it comes to making a positive identification. Swallows, especially tree swallows, have already commenced migration southward; a few cliff and barn swallows remain and were probably late in brooding young. Nighthawk migration is nearly complete, and their call on warm summer evenings in the city will soon become but a memory. The late-nesting goldfinches exhibit a sense of urgency as they feed their young, the last of the season's songbirds to hatch. Thistle down, their preferred nest lining material, wasn't available until the early part of August. The mature thistle seed is also an important food source and is fed to the young by the parents in the form of a regurgitated "soup."

As the length of daylight coincides with springtime hours, confusing signals are sent to both plant and animals. Frogs may begin to sing from shallow woodland ponds and some birds might start setting up territo-

Milkweed pods opening to release seeds on the wind.

ries and check out suitable birdhouses. This reaction a part of photoperiodism and is displayed by some plants as well, causing them to send forth autumn blossoms like those of May.

Garden flowers are at their peak bloom as are the late-blooming summer wildflowers. In marshy areas, the prolific blooming orange, spotted jewelweed provides a nectar banquet for migrating ruby throated hummingbirds, who will need to maintain the layer of fat acquired before leaving the boreal forests.

This is the time to harvest summer's bounty. Ripening wild grapes, an autumn treat not only for crows, woodducks, and several species of songbirds, but for us as well while we wait for the kiss of frost to seal the fruit with sweetness. Wild plums and domestic apples of all varieties are ripening and will soon fill bushel baskets. Gooseberries, especially the smooth purple-black variety, are ready to be made into a delicious jam. The mature fruit of staghorn sumac bear small hairs containing malic acid, the same chemical found in unripe apples. When several heads are picked, swirled in a Mason jar full of water for about ten minutes, the water-soluble acid produces a tart, pale-pink liquid. After straining through cheese clothe to remove the hairs, the mixture is sweetened to taste and, poured over ice, results in a tasty lemonade. The ripe red fruit of buffaloberry can be made into a jam, but is more of an epicurean treat for cedar waxwings. Migrating robins as well as other songbirds seek out the abundant orange fruit hanging from mountain ash and consume the tiny apples from crab apple trees. Grains and wild rice are ready for harvest, while milkweed pods continue to swell with tomorrow's progeny.

What sign of autumn would be complete without commenting on hornets and angry honeybees that, knowing their days are numbered, are starting to develop their fall "attitude." In Minnesota, August is the month for the most reported stings by insects of the order Hymenoptera. Just opening a can of pop or trying to enjoy a piece of fruit outdoors enmeshes a person in a combat zone. The worker honeybees are depleting their glycogen reserve stored in the wing muscles. Recently it has been reported that this energy source is good for only 500 miles and, with or without a frost, they will succumb when they hit "empty." The queens of both species will, of course, survive and be around to perpetuate the next generation.

The sulphur shelf, one of Minnesota's "fool-proof four" mushrooms, heralds the advent of autumn fungi feasts. Commonly found in deciduous forests, it can be found growing on either basswood or oak tree trunks. When prepared with a coating of flour and sauteed in butter, it is not unlike chicken both in flavor and texture. Meanwhile, in northern forests, red squirrels begin to harvest their mushrooms, caching them securely in tree branches to air dry for consumption during the lean months of winter.

With the conclusion of August, the season of sweet sadness begins, for everything is winding down for another year. There will be dormancy, and frosts will end summer flowers, but the brilliance of other fall colors will gently ease us into winter's beauty once again.

14

Allis and the Apprentice

Her demeanor was cold and indifferent, and I had been forewarned of her temperamental personality. In her fifties, she was known to be a stubborn gal, but I needed her assistance—she was all I had. "She" was a 5,000-pound tractor, an ancient Allis Chalmers. We became better acquainted before my husband departed on a two-week business trip. After only thirty minutes on the job training with my mentor, I knew what would make Allis purr like a kitten and run like a tiger. The purpose of this introduction was in case our quarter-mile driveway drifted shut; I would be able to plow myself out with the aid of Allis's front-end loader.

I eased the car onto the snow-covered county road. The snow-dusted freeway, albeit intermittently slippery, was typical for a January day in Minnesota. What wasn't normal, however, was finding the car totally covered with snow in a covered parking ramp after work! This was an ominous indicator of what winds might have done to our driveway in the open country. There, tall marshland grasses, acting like natural snow fencing entrapped blowing snow, but billowing leftovers always settled in the driveway. While the radio reported a pleasant thirty-three degrees above zero, the strong southeast wind swirled the snow in every direction and dropped the wind chill well below zero. My heart sank as I approached the driveway entrance, noting how the snow was whipped like cream into two-foot high drifts blending into the adjacent field.

After turning off the highway, I judiciously abandoned the car in the first two-foot snowdrift encountered. Every winter, in spite of a snow fence, this driveway presented a challenge following snowfalls with high winds. If this car were to see the inside of the garage, I would have to fire up old Allis. After high stepping it through deep snow to the house, I took our two dogs for a not so ordinary walk down the driveway. Quickly, the tenacious quality of the snow rolled snowballs up in the long, flowing coat of our shih tzu. These spheres grew to the size of baseballs with occasional golfballs in between, and totally packed his undercarriage. Bucking like a fifteen-pound midget bronco, he finally lumbered into the house for a therapeutic "deballing." The hair dryer seemed a likely choice for a rapid melt, but snow doesn't liquefy as quickly as it compacts, and, besides, Allis was beckoning during the last hour of sunlight. Quickly I stashed the small dog in the bathtub to thaw and prepared to meet my challenge. For this middle-aged suburbanite with near zero mechanical skill and absolutely no knowledge of heavy machinery, I had my work cut out for me. Confidently I marched outside with the house-warmed battery.

The battery cables were stiff and balked at being attached to the proper poles. Tightening down the nuts with the wrench soon became an electrifying experience as sparks flew in one direction and I in the other. With trepidation I cautiously continued and, being a veteran now, merely flinched when the second set of fireworks illuminated my work area. Now was the moment of truth. Would the tractor start when I pulled the starter simultaneously with the choke?

It didn't even turn over.

Undaunted, I prepared a new strategy. Adeptly now, I readjusted the cables and tightened more securely. The positive pole's cable was particularly stubborn but was eased more firmly into place with a hammer! Friendly persuasion works every time. Funny, it looked so easy two days previously when I received instructions from my husband, now in Alaska. As I eased myself into the floppy metal seat, cushioned with an old pillow, I could feel that this time ancient Allis would fire, and she did! Somehow, by process of elimination, my fingers found their way to the ignition switch (which also doubled as a light switch—the logic of which still escapes me.) The beautiful rumbling purr of ignition was abruptly interrupted by the explosion of the pop can lifting off the vertical exhaust pipe (I forgot step number one in tractor starting: "Remove the pop can.") Noting the aerodynamic landing of the pop can, I pushed in the clutch, shifted into first, let out the clutch, and I was rolling.

And hey! This was fun, a piece of cake—all these levers, pedals, and a whatchamacallit that really made no sense. I couldn't remember in what order any of these things were to be operated. I motored down the driveway feeling like a teenager experiencing her first trip alone in the family car. A push off into the field here and there with Allis's front-end loader and the road would be cleared in a jiffy. However, turning the 5,000-pound beast in deep snow was another story and "pushing off" was not as easy as it had been on the practice run on packed snow. Quickly a six-foot mountain sprung up in front of the front-end loader, and, being immovable, the engine killed. Effortlessly I flooded the engine and, for the coup de grace, ran the battery down as the sun set on the wintry landscape. With the skill of a surgeon now, I removed Allis' now defunct life support and carried the battery back for an overnight revitalization. Knowing that we had a battery charger was my last ray of hope. The next day, Saturday, meant that, with a recharged battery, I would have all weekend to accomplish my task. I had visions of my pride—not to mention my husband's—if I could get the darn driveway cleared. After reading all instructions for the charger and completing the final step, a high pitched squeal shrieked through the house as the Amp needle went into death throes, landing on zero and taking my last scintilla of confidence with it.

Over two thousand miles away, my husband must have felt a twinge of extra sensory panic. He called within the hour. Trying to sound optimistic, he hoped to hear a rave revue of my debut as "Snowplow Lady Exceptional." Instead he learned of near electrocution and a defeated ego. After commiserating with me and offering suggestions, he renewed my spirit for Round II.

Dawn brought minus twenty-two degrees Fahrenheit, but, with the theme from "Rocky" in the back of mind, I started to walk down the driveway with Allis' recharged battery. Around the bend I encountered new drifts from the previous night's additional snow and high winds. In town the wind velocity had been reported as thirty-seven miles per hour; in wind-chill terms that translated to minus fifty-three degrees. By comparison, in the open countryside, the metropolitan zephyrs almost sounded balmy compared to the near ground blizzard swirling around me. This new obstacle called for a change of navigational gear; now snowshoes were necessary for walking, and the toboggan had to come down from the rafters to transport the battery and snow shovel. When I approached the tractor and assessed my predicament, I found that my mountain of snow had petrified overnight. To ask Allis to move aside this mini Alps with her bucket might stress the hydraulic lift mechanism. With frustration as my fuel, I shoveled aside rigid chunks of snow forming the barrier in

Crystalline sundown viewed through a frosty window belies the temperature of minus twenty degrees on the snowshoes outside.

front of our car. Depositing the battery and hooking up the cables was a cinch when, as my instructor said, "The cable goes on easily when correctly turned right side up." No hammer necessary for this round. The projectile, also known as the pop can, was removed before it could launch into a distant snowbank.

With the aplomb of a tiller of the land, I mounted my tractor, came up with the magical combination to bring about ignition and was off and plowing. However, the continuing drop in temperature plus the gusty northwest wind further plummeted the wind chill factor and froze the drifts to concrete consistency. With the car parked in front of me and a mountain range behind me, there was no where to go but off in the field to turn around and hit the wall head on, as they say. The field snow depth defied the chained tractor wheels, and soon I was spinning on frozen ground, mulching last summer's grasses into a brown blizzard. Thus concluded Round II of plowing, without accomplishing much except freezing my derriere (forgot my pillow for the metal tractor seat!). Admitting defeat and conceding to Boreas, I hastily retreated to the warmth of the fireplace and a glass of wine to assuage my wounded ego.

The car would have to survive another minus twenty-two-degree predicted low for the night as well as another week and a half at the end of the driveway until my husband returned. Garbage cans rode to the edge of the highway on the toboggan. Bringing in gro-

Frost patterns form a miniature forest on the windows.

103

ceries in paper bags with handles brought disaster as seams gave way, sending apples rolling across the frozen tundra, to be quickly passed up by the feather-weight roll of paper towels. In my favor was that we owned large backpacks—blaze orange ones that glowed like beacons in the middle of the snowy field? As I foraged for my groceries strewn over the snowdrifts, I wondered what passing motorists thought of this floundering image towing a pack-laden toboggan with one hand and groping in the snow with the other.

The positive side to this misadventure—5:30 A.M. snowshoe walks to the car under a full moon revealed snow glittering like diamond dust while tree shadows danced upon its surface. By moonlight, new messages had been inscribed on fresh snow—like a chalkboard—detailing the previous night's activities. Tiny mouse tracks etched a trailing pattern of tatting as they made short forays above snow; heart shaped imprints of inquisitive deer near the house as they traveled to their corn feeder, the spore of opportunistic fox and then, those crazy rabbits that must have partied all night. The silence is interrupted only by snowshoes crunching upon the snow and the sound of the territorial hooting of the great horned owls that would soon begin nesting.

The day before my husband returned, the United Parcel Service left a terse note in our mailbox stating: "Please plow driveway for delivery."

The . . . delivery item? A Prairie Home Companion's selection of cassette tapes. For this diminutive item, less than sixteen ounces, I was supposed to plow the driveway? Granted, a collection of Garrison Keillor's cassette tapes from Minnesota's mythical Lake Wobegon was special. But if the deliveryman only knew how much I had tried to clear that blasted road, he would have sent Mr. Keillor himself in via dog sled!

As I plunged through knee deep snow toward our abode, my near maniacal laughter intensified as I reread the request from the ever competent UPS and thought, *Garrison Keillor, have I got a tale for you!*

15

Canine Constitutionals

For each dog, every chance to go for a walk with its owner is like a first-time event. Each opportunity is greeted with relentless enthusiasm for an outing sure to guarantee new adventure with potential for a myriad of discoveries and scents to be deciphered. And, if there is a feral cat to be treed, well then, there is a real sense of accomplishment and purpose! Whereas our dogs put on nothing more than a happy expression to go for a walk, I must dress for all extremes of weather. But I, too, must admit I look forward to these walks and delight in new seasonal discoveries, visual or auditory.

Not only have "the boys" treed growling baby raccoons, scolding squirrels, and chattering chipmunks, they have sent bewildered woodchucks (yes, they do climb trees when they have a ninety-five-pound retriever on their tail) scrambling up any nearby sapling. There have been encounters of tenderness with wildlife during outdoor excursions that have become indelibly etched in our special memories. Such as the time our golden retriever discovered a fawn, just hours old and which had become separated from its mother. Our dog, the ever-playful "Buck," thought he had found a new playmate and tried to elicit a response. Assuming his best invitational play posture—his paws stretched within a

Nature dictated that this fawn lie still in spite of a clumsy golden retriever's invitation to play.

Rusty, our first golden retriever.

few inches of the fawn's nose, his fanny held high in the air while his tail furiously gyrated to near "lift-off" momentum—he gently lifted one paw several times and slapped it just short of touching the moist black nose. But the little, tightly coiled bundle of soft brown fur dappled with white spots was too frightened and remained still, as nature had dictated. It tucked its nose even further under its foreleg. As quickly as this event occurred, we interrupted, fearing the young animal would become too stressed. Within moments of leaving the area, I heard its mother give a loud "huff" and saw the little fawn jump up and bound towards her, emitting joyous bleats in anticipation of their reunion.

Then there was the gentle encounter between the big, clumsy retriever and a baby robin. The feathered ball of fluff had fledged prematurely into an uncertain world when it fluttered down in the middle of our path. Normally aggressive, our game-bird hunting dog gently nosed the beady-eyed lump and then looked up at me with a quizzical expression, accentuated by alternating arching eyebrows. He looked back down at the little bird and then touched its beak with his nose before proudly prancing away as his mistress assured him this was the right thing to do.

But sometimes during our walks, the roles have been reversed, and the dogs become the subjects of pursuit! In the bird world, not only can several species lead a dog away from its young by feigning a broken wing, they can charge with full vengeance while emitting raging screams to divert attention from their flightless brood. Several times we have encountered a very protective mother ruffed grouse who was not impressed by the size of the retriever and charged very aggressively. Even small muskrats have a temperament that, when challenged, will aggressively charge not only the dogs but humans as well. Skunks? Well, that's another story, and the recipient of the sulphurous perfume deserved it.

So many walks, so many memories that some seem to blend, but an occasional walk stands out because of a special event, such as a particularly beautiful sunrise or wildlife sighting and, when in combination, it is spectacular. Such as one cold January morning in Minnesota, the rambunctious golden retriever and exuberant shih tzu, knowing nothing of wind chills, raced circles around me as soon as my foot slipped into one of my winter boots. When the chaos at the door became only mild congestion, I braced myself for the explosion of the retriever trying to propel himself through the door before I could get it open. Stepping outside, I was immediately embraced by the frigid cold morning air, becoming inspired to walk most briskly to jump-start my circulation. The dogs were already bounding ahead of me down the dirt road, inhaling the scent left behind by the night creatures, big or small—to them it all appeared to be very fascinating!

This morning adventure began with a spectacular sunrise of flaming reds and burnished oranges washing across the sky, turning the fringes of the clouds in the west a vivid pink contrasting against the still gray-blue of early dawn. The staccato reverberance of a pileated woodpecker echoed across the field, emanating from the depths of the forest where huge dead elms provided just the perfect instrument from which to announce its territorial presence. From afar, a great horned owl called its trisyllabic hoot as an accompaniment. In the distance, a late browsing white-tailed deer slowly raised its head, looked at us and then faded into the forest long before the dogs could catch sight or scent. As we entered a clump of sapling oak trees, a startled barred owl rose reluctantly from the forest floor and perched in a small red oak, perhaps hesitant to leave the area because we interrupted its morning mouse catch. With its large, dark-brown eyes—appearing the color of coal-black in the low light of early morning—it watched the dogs with a penetrating, alien-like gaze as they traversed its hunting grounds. Fluffing and rearranging its cross-barred gray plumage, it looked even larger and allowed me to approach within twenty feet of the tree before I turned, diverting the dogs to an alternate path. When I looked back, the owl had, characteristically, silently disappeared. What a phenomenal visual reward for taking the "boys" for their morning walk! I had seen captive barred owls in the past, but to see one in the wild was very special indeed.

Later, as the warming rays of sunlight cascaded down tree trunks, black-capped chickadees tumbled from their nighttime roost, flitting through a maze of branches and busily greeting the new day with their cheery "dee–dee" call. Bluejays by contrast, nosily greeted the dawn, and one is already perfecting its "pump-handle" call used for spring courtship. As we continued on, the shih tzu deviated from the path and waded through deep snow to inspect a sooty gray patch of rodent fur at the base of buffaloberry bushes. Looking about for the rest of the body, I wondered if this was the result of a kill made by a northern shrike. Occasionally these black-masked songbirds with raptor like behavior migrate south to central Minnesota in winter. Typically, because the shrike's feet are too weak to hold its prey down during consumption, they will impale insects or mice on thorns or sharp spikes such as those on the bufalloberry shrub and dine from this position. But before I could evaluate the fur, the small dog inhaled the evidence, and we continued our walk for more dog treasures—such as deer droppings and rabbit raisins, the caviar of the dog world. No amount of scolding ccould correct this habit and, hey, rabbits consumed their own droppings, so they had to be good!

From the south end of the property, a ring-necked pheasant crowed. It was reassuring that at least one had survived the winter thus far after their numbers plummeted in this area during the devastating winter of 1997. It was doubly rewarding to hear a rooster because the previous summer we raised and released a batch of pheasants. I hoped this was one of our birds augmenting its diet with corn from our five-acre food plot for wildlife.

An interesting aspect of these constitutionals has been the observation of territorial or dominance behavior when with two dogs of considerable size difference.

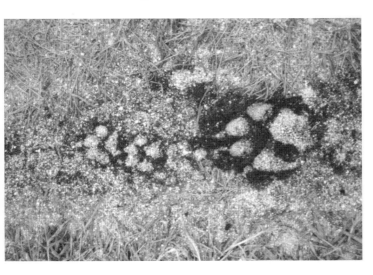

Canine prints embossed in mud and dusted with snow.

109

Just as with wolves, the higher one can "mark" or uri-
nate on a tree, the more dominant the animal; a shih tzu
doesn't stand a chance, and it appeared the retriever
delighted in negating any territorial marking the little
guy made. Another behavior I had only observed in
white-tailed deer was that of foot stomping the ground
when it was nervous, possibly sensing danger. When
our retriever encountered a large bullsnake, he, too, ner-
vously stamped the ground a safe distance from the reptile. During the egg-laying season of painted turtles,
when they were on land searching for sandy soils, they
become delightful play objects when the dogs encounter
them on our walks, necessitating diversionary tactics to
insure the slow-moving reptiles' safety. One behavior
particularly touched me and caused me to wonder how
a dog interprets another animal's death in the wild. One
afternoon the retriever discovered a dead, juvenile raccoon in the marsh. After much investigation, he came
back to me and sat. Sitting beside me, he pricked up his
ears and looked up with questioning eyes and then
back at the raccoon and again, back at me. This went
on several minutes, the whole time he displayed a
degree of anxiety and confusion, perhaps wondering
why this animal didn't move. Only after much coaxing,
were we able to leave the area and continue our walk.

The joy of owning a dog and taking it for walks
is a privilege, and to enjoy nature along the way is a
bonus. Occasionally I have been reluctant to take "the
boys" for their walk because of the weather, but they
convince me otherwise with those expressive, pleading
eyes that say there are rabbits to be chased, roosters to
be flushed, and thirteen-striped ground squirrels to be
tormented. A dog seems to know when its human companion is in need of at least one constitutional a day!
They seem to know a chance to unwind after work, to
run and play and to get down to their level is a stress
reliever for their owner. This quality time of companion-
ship is not only beneficial to both parties mentally and
physically, it intensifies the bond between them.

16

The Winter of Discontent

Not only will the winter of 1997 be ingrained in the memory of many mid-westerners—and in my mind particularly—it marks a haunting revelation of the struggle for wildlife survival, most notable, that of the white-tailed deer. On our acreage, the Farm, in west-central Minnesota, their plight was all too visible and disturbing. Some say it is Nature's way of culling the herd; only the strongest will survive and perpetuate future generations. But witnessing starvation in the aftermath of multiple blizzards and limited access to food tugged at my heart strings more than any normal sequence of events.

As the wildlife sought shelter to await their fate, we, too, found ourselves challenged as the first January blizzard struck, setting the stage for a winter seemingly without end. Ironically, our mini-vacation over New Year's started out unseasonably mild and required only a lightweight woolen sweater while snowshoeing. The warmth even coaxed a stonefly to take wing from the nearby gurgling stream and to bask upon the snow. I found the forest silent and disappointingly void of wildlife. Only the crunch of my snowshoes on the snow penetrated the balmy winter air. Deer tracks criss-crossed, weaving an infinite labyrinth throughout the woodland. A solitary downy woodpecker suddenly

111

tapped out a repetitious, monotone resonance as it probed a grub dinner from the old, gray elm tree. Squirrels as well as deer had skeletonized cobs of corn taken from our wildlife food plot before discarding them haphazardly throughout the forest. Mentally, I compared this "trashing" of the snow-covered landscape to that of human delinquents who littered their own highways. The fox I had heard barking in the pastel sunrise had left only its spore neatly imprinted in a meandering fashion as it no doubt searched, listening for that unwary vole or deer mouse traveling throughout cozy subnivian runways. Throughout western Minnesota the barometric pressure dropped with the onslaught of yet another impending blizzard; the snow was already very deep, making hunting difficult for predators such as the fox. Sadly, survival for "slyboots" would come only to the most cunning; perhaps luck would be a contributing factor that day.

As I continued my quest for an unknown highlight, photographic or otherwise, I discovered at the base of a partially hollowed-out basswood bole a cottontail rabbit hunched up as though cold. The photographer in me thought she had finally found a critter to photograph. Carefully, I removed the lens cover from the camera while I slowly advanced toward the immobile subject. But something was wrong. The frigid pose was too rigid; it was rigor mortis. The gray, glazed coloring of the eyes confirmed it. Perhaps the rabbit was old, sick or both and sought shelter during a previous sub-zero night and never awakened. A peaceful death for a small mammal having a high mortality rate in Nature's contest of predator versus prey.

As I approached the murmuring hillside spring that sent mini-torrents through moss-covered rocks before wending its way through the marsh and flowing into the lake, I saw that deer had left their signature in and upon the snow as they had enjoyed winter's gift of flowing spring water. Unbelievably, upon a branch of a sapling, a spider climbed up a spoke of its web. Its movement was somewhat lethargic; that it was moving at all probably reflected the radiating warmth generated by the open spring.

Exiting the forest, my thoughts were of the rabbit, pondering the nature of its demise. Not a photograph was snapped, but the snowshoe excursion had invigorated my body as well as my soul. Taking a shortcut through the six-foot-tall prairie bluestem grass, I saw the familiar scene of tree sparrows doing their bungee-cord jumping thing as they rode the seed-bearing stems to ground level. This clever maneuver allowed them to pluck the minute seeds from the delicate spikelet located at the very tip. Finding this avian carnival performance amusing, I stopped for a few minutes to watch about two dozen of these winter migrants from the Canadian Arctic as they bobbed up and down at various intervals before their descent to dine.

After I returned to the comfort of the cabin, the temperature began to drop, the wind increased, and sleet began to fall rapidly, encasing everything in ice. By

Two white-tailed deer gaze at the photographer from "their" corn food plot.

the time the storm finally subsided, everything would be covered with one-half inch of ice and buried under twenty-one inches of snow that drifted as high as six feet. While we enjoyed the warmth of a wood stove, the wildlife had to curl up tighter and bury their noses deeper in the warmth of their winter coats.

A month later when the weather had moderated, another snowshoe outing, in contrast to the one before the storm, was teeming with wildlife, white-tailed deer being the most prevalent. The plethora of their tracks led to the corn food plot containing about twenty hungry deer happily gleaning corn. The combination of a 500 mm lens plus a 2X extender and comfortable weather provided for a memorable photo opportunity, causing me to conclude that some deer are pretty and some are, well, just plain homely. Perhaps it was a feminist thought, but I speculated that the homely ones were the bucks, having lost their antlers. Then there was the question of savvy; some were either smart, dumb or insanely curious. The latter conclusion was made when a deer advanced straight toward me within thirty feet, making the high-tech camera gear almost unnecessary. But mostly, to get their attention, I had to whistle, whoop and holler, causing them to be totally mystified by my unhumanly "predator" behavior. At this stage of winter they were not stressed; they seemed bright eyed and for the most part, wary.

As winter deepened and several more blizzards drove through the area, the deer, up to thirty or more methodically scoured the corn food plot at all hours of the day and night, even bedded down in the middle of it to be near their food source. Now, we began to find dead pheasants and signs of other wildlife suffering. Finding the cornfield stripped, my husband drove fifty miles round trip to purchase five hundred pounds of corn. He put this in several large feeders. It was but a small portion of their needs.

Our five-acre corn food plot—sometimes cost-shared with the Department of Natural Resources—temporarily helped other wildlife as well. A small flock of pheasants—evidenced by characteristic tracks and occasional flushes—three species of squirrels, innumerable rodents, and non-migrating birds, most notably bluejays and woodpeckers were also enjoying the corn. When the corn was gone, the white-tailed deer turned their attention to our mixed forest of LTA (Limited Term Agreement) evergreens planted twenty years previously. They clearly favored white pine, but red pine, spruce, and, surprisingly, jackpine and even native junipers were stripped where our trail gave them easy access to the trees. Their droppings soon revealed the low nutritional value of evergreens, looking more like coarse wood fiber pellets. Even our two dogs that, like most of their kind, had the disgusting tendency to consider deer droppings a delicacy, ignored the buff-colored pellets.

The first deer causality we saw was discovered not more than thirty yards from the cabin. A victim of a predator, the tracks were inconclusive because of previous melting and wind-blown snow, but there was a high probability of a coyote or two as the perpetrators. It was a very depressing sight, not just the kill, but the emaciation and lack of tallow that confirmed that the deer were indeed starving. The golden retriever approached the carcass, circled and then returned to my side before sitting down; with his ears pricked up, he studied the scene and looked up at me with questioning eyes and then again looked at the doe. I had seen this behavior in the past when we encountered the dead raccoon. The dog seemed strangely pensive, almost reverent, and I resisted an attempt to anthromorphosize his reaction. As winter wore on and daylight lengthened, it brought promise, but the deer wandered aimlessly and constantly, burning up valuable calories they could ill afford to squander. Some even seemed to lose their fear of man, staring balefully like domestic cattle and roaming the frozen lake surface in small herds.

When the long winter finally abated, melting snow revealed the body count. The experts were right.

Mostly fawns were found, but yearlings as well and probably those that went into winter in marginal health had succumbed. Even making the rounds in early spring while closing bluebird houses on our bluebird trail revealed more bodies. A very sad statement signifying a very bad winter experienced by humans and beasts throughout the Midwest.

In the far north, the severity of the winter was slightly less than the previous year, but the winter was no less of a challenge for survival. In the normal balance of predator versus prey, the timber wolf plays an important role as evidenced by a discovery we made in early April. While walking along the shore, my husband noticed a "shed," or so he thought, a single antler resting on the still frozen lake surface. An antler is always an object of curiosity and a find that makes an outing special. However, upon closer inspection, the shed was only part of the story. Brushing away the snow, the other antler was barely visible through the opaque slush ice. Upon looking around the site, he noticed a spinal column and part of a large leg bone. Thus the scene was most likely a wolf kill. My husband then walked back to get the chain saw, reasoning we could simply slice through the ice and recover the antlers. Finding the ice thicker than anticipated, we fired up the auger used for drilling holes for ice fishing. With overlapping cuts while circumnavigating the antler, chipping at the additional ten inches of solid ice with another part of ice fishing gear known as a "spud" and sheer determination, the block of ice was freed and bobbed to the surface. We had the entire head with the matching large antler, a beautiful, massively beamed, ten-point "rack." Delicately chipping the ice with the spud freed the individual tines and revealed interesting details. Clearly this was a wolf kill, but we wondered how an animal with this large of a rack, usually indicative of good nutrition and health, could become prey. As we admired the rack, we noticed bright red blood flowing from two deep, penetrating fang wounds on the beam, and the tip of the antler that

Deep winter snows in the north can be beautiful but deadly for the white-tailed deer and other wildlife.

had been beneath the ice was broken off and still oozing blood as well. We surmised that, after the wolves had pursued the buck in deep snow, the animal was exhausted by the time it reached the lake. Perhaps some pack members attacked from the rear and possibly the leader of the pack sank its fangs into the antler as the buck lowered its head to fend off his attacker from the front. With a twisting motion and all of the wolf's weight now on the antler, the buck stumbled. With the fall, the fight for survival was lost.

This was but probably one of many similar scenarios played out many times throughout the winter across the North Country. There are those who would condemn the wolf for its part in the drama, but it represents the balance of nature, and it is necessary. Unlike the white-tailed deer in west-central Minnesota that slowly starved to death, this animal's demise was relatively quick.

17

Winter's Silent Beauty

Barring a freak twenty-nine-inch snowstorm like we endured on Halloween 1991 that lengthened the season dramatically, Minnesota guarantees six months of crystalline beauty, beauty that comes in many forms from the geometric design of a stellar, dendritic snowflake of temperate snowfalls to delicate fronds on a frosty window pane to marvelous wind-whipped ice sculptures in the open fields and woods.

As winter unofficially commences, the thermometer begins its downward spiral in November, a month characterized by the *Gashkadino Giziz*, Objibwe for Freezing Moon, a time of transition where colliding air masses produce sleet that can be deadly or beautiful. When it is the latter, the landscape becomes entombed in a glaze of sparkling ice. Grasses, having stood tall through autumn gales, glisten like spun gold or glitter like beads on a crystal chandelier, while wildflower seed heads become glassine works of art.

Sculpted by Nature, icicles glow at sundown.

If the air is calm, December's combination of low stratus clouds, moisture-laden fog, and temperatures near freezing can produce a magical fairyland of frost. Like the quills on a porcupine's back, delicate needles of hoarfrost sprout from everything. Even more dramatic is rime frost that is harder and denser than hoarfrost and often occurs on the windward side of anything stationary, spreading a spectacular frosting over the region.

Hoarfrost on the branches of pine (above) and crabapple (right) soften the lines of winter, making a fairyland of field and forest.

On such a day in late December with a temperature hovering near thirty degrees Fahrenheit in central Minnesota, the countryside became adorned with a veil of white frosting, creating a magical fairyland. Long needles of hoarfrost grew from every object, whether natural or man-made, leaving one nearly breathless with the resulting incredible beauty. Like a child about to experience the season's first snowfall, I couldn't wait to go outside and enjoy Nature's artistry and decipher messages inscribed upon the snow-covered landscape.

Crystalline ice encasing the previous summer's browned flower stem sparkles like rhinestone jewelry.

My walk began by crossing fields containing last summer's wildflower seed heads now blooming in a unison of white elegance. Wending my way down to our marsh, I noted an abundance of activity. Deer in search of their daily eight pounds of browse had created a labyrinth of trails. A meadow vole with dark-gray, velvety fur emerged from its subnivian world and scurried above ground with the confused coordination of a wind-up, mechanical toy. Dainty paw prints by the bubbling spring confirmed that a mink had discovered the previous day's offering of minnows left from ice fishing.

121

Not far from its winter den where muddied tracks led, fox spore punctuated the ice-encrusted flowage and dissolved into the cattails. Before entering the forest, I noticed wild grapevines entwined in the low-hanging limbs of a poplar tree. The vine still held last summer's fruit and ice encased the grape clusters. Freezing had ruptured some of the grapes, tinting the crystallized snow a delicate shade of lavender. Not far from this momentary distraction, ruffed grouse tracks sauntered up the hillside, leaving a trail of nibbled basswood seedling bud scales littering the snow. The winter growth of a horny fringe around the grouse's toes created miniature snowshoes, enabling it to traverse soft snow effortlessly. A large fox squirrel seemed oblivious to my presence and continued to busily extract a snack from last autumn's acorn cache. Even a sleepy striped skunk had awakened from its winter nap during this bonus warm spell to meander about leaving its telltale tracks in the snow. Flocks of chickadees seemed to be gathering for a convention, while goldfinches flew overhead whispering soft twitters. Redpoll finches tumbled out of the leaden sky like snowflakes blushed with the rose shading of a sunrise and landed momentarily to decorate frosty red pine boughs, creating a scene for a Christmas card painting. Just as quickly as they landed, they were off again on the never-ending quest for scarce winter food. The little downy woodpeckers busily searched tree boles for a meal while performing stylized acrobatics and uttering an occasional impatient "pik."

Continuing my walk through the woods, I couldn't help but think that the leather bindings on my snowshoes rubbing against my rubber boots sounded like the squeak of a mouse. I stopped several times to give my best imitation of a mouse by kissing the back of my hand. Waiting several minutes before proceeding on, I hoped the combination of "squeaks" just might convince either a screech owl or saw-whet owl that dinner was on the way. Perhaps I'd catch sight of one or the other. I would gladly have taken any pose with the camera that

hung from my neck like an accessory appendage—
always at the ready to capture Nature's offering.

I have come to the conclusion that I am addicted
to my camera, sort of like the American Express card—
"Don't leave home without it." But on this day I left
behind the strobe and macro lens—a decision I would
regret. My wandering down the timber trail took me
past a huge dead elm entwined with brilliant orange bittersweet. The fruit, long ago popped open by the first
frost, glowed against the leaden, winter sky. Crystalline
hoarfrost filagreed their petal-like seed capsules—just
gorgeous, but a photo possibility was doubtful. I wres-
tled with a deadfall amongst the tangled understory for
a better angle. I snapped branches noisily and, in retro-
spect, created quite a ruckus. Still looking for a better
angle, I moved to the right side of the tree. And there it
was. A saw-whet owl!

It sat calmly gazing down at this noisy *Homo
sapien,* who had invaded its quiet forest. I froze in my
tracks. I wanted to use my camera, but instead, I just
stared and marveled at the eight-inch feathered mite. If
nothing else, I wanted to commit this memory to permanent storage. Like a greeting card, the owl, too, was surrounded with a circular segment of the spiked, inch-
long hoarfrost-laden bittersweet vine. Underneath the
small buff-colored talons lay a white-footed mouse that
would become its dinner. As we continued to stare at
each other, I wondered if direct eye contact was threat-
ening to such a small owl and if it might attack. For a
moment I was glad I wore my glasses! I felt my own
eyes open wider as I stared at the owl's golden, hypnot-
ic, dilated eyes. We look into the depths of each other's
soul. But at the same time, I found this creature somewhat comical, like a caricature of a little preacher in a
pulpit as it looked down at its appreciative audience of
one. With feathers seemingly slicked straight back over
its head, it looked like a Brill Cream ad!

I snapped my one and only picture—the lighting
was poor and it was the end of the roll. And darn, I

didn't have another roll of film! However, I continued to study this diminutive ball of fluff as it nodded off with boredom, still clutching its mouse. What a spectacular conclusion to this snowshoe walk! So much beauty abounds if we just journey outdoors and enjoy this special time of the year instead of counting the days until the first spring crocus appears.

By January, solidly frozen lakes reveal subtle beauty in the form of columns of gas bubbles trapped in black ice. And once, while crossing a stream on a bril-

A trio of imprints representing motion have left behind distinct signatures in the snow: the parallel tracks of skis with an oak leaf imprint superimposed on them and next to the imprints of deer hooves.

liantly clear but cold day, I encountered beautiful ice crystals in the shape of large petals forming elegant "blooming" frost flowers upon the frozen surface. In the fading light of sundown, a glint of captured sunshine winked back at me as the wind riffled individual florets, and I remembered thinking what exquisite and intricately rare beauty had been created. Following the same stream to the lake, I discovered stalagmite formations along the shore, attesting to a turbulent freeze-up as waves froze and accumulated upon the rocks. As I returned home, rays from the low winter sun crept ever further into the house through south-facing windows, creating a shaft of sunlight piercing through the aquarium water, projecting a spectacular rainbow of colors on the electric stove burner coils.

Mid-February, still caught in winter's grasp, could not defeat the height of the sun's penetrating rays. Snow melted even though the temperature remained below freezing. On sunlit western-exposed boulders, drop upon drop of ice melt created a sphere of frozen motion, crystalline icicles glittering with intense clarity as they cascaded from lichen-covered outcroppings.

Soon, as the warmth of the March sun intensified, icicles born overnite turn cloudy, causing them to shed tears in the heat of the next day, while the dripping of melting roof-top snow brought soothing music to the ears awaiting the sounds of spring. The muffled sound of awakening streams, as they gurgled beneath the slowly shrinking blanket of snow covering the landscape, was one of affirmation.

But wait! April was a capricious and unpredictable lady. Like November, early April spelled a transitional weather month; cold Canadian air masses could clash with warm fronts from the south. A fleeting sleet storm could once more turn the countryside into a glistening wonderland of ice even as spring dethroned winter from beneath.

We knew winter was truly over when the lake ice turned gray and began to break-up. In high winds, the ice might be violently tossed upon the shore in huge slabs, sometimes piling as high as a house on the shores of larger lakes. Or, on the other hand, ice could depart magically, without a trace. Several times, while canoeing the open portions of a lake on a warm afternoon in April, I have heard the crystalline tinkling of thousands of tiny bells as small shards of ice gently collided with one another. The beauty, no longer silent, had a sound unlike any other and cast a spell over the participant in Nature's arena. Fragmenting further, the ice swirled into an eddy created by slicing the canoe paddle through the water and, seemingly, tiny particles dissolved and dipped below the lake surface.

The promise of rebirth of another spring had begun. Just as in the metamorphosis of the cecropia moth, the pupa within the silken, gray cocoon could break forth at any moment. Blow gentle breezes, blow, for the door for spring's entrance stood ajar. Returning migrants poised, ready. We who live in the North Country awaited the next scene in the theater of seasons!

Cecropia moth cocoon on a twig with new spring leaves.

About the Author

An avid outdoor person, a self-taught naturalist, photographer, and writer, Minnesota-born Barbara Mulvaney grew up in Vancouver, Washington. She returned to Minnesota to attend the University of Minnesota and pursued a career in Cytotechnology. With training completed in Rochester at the Mayo Clinic, she then worked in Minneapolis hospitals for nearly thirty-five years and co-founded the Minnesota Society of Cytology. She also is a founding member of both the Freshwater Biological Institute and the Minnesota Wildlife Heritage Foundation. She,  along with her husband, Bruce, is a member of the Bluebird Recovery Program and collect data from seventy-five nest boxes on their Gilchrist Lake property, as well as from the bluebird trail they are establishing in Glacial Lakes State Park. She is a member of the National Wildlife Federation and the Pope County Humane Society, a volunteer for the Minnesota Department of Natural Resources, and a member of Retired and Senior Volunteer Program (delivering Meals-on-Wheels). Her photos have appeared in numerous publications, including *Minnesota Weatherguide* Calenders (1986, 1988, 1990, 1991, 1993, 1995–2001), the *Minnesota Volunteer* (1981, 1996–1998), *Birds and Blooms* (June/July 1995 and October/November 1995), and the covers of *Minnesota Medicine* (1988), *Wisconsin Natural Resources* (October 1989), *Maple Grove Residents Guide* (1991).